WALKING IN THE WOODS

Walking *in the* Woods
A MÉTIS MEMOIR
HERB BELCOURT

BRINDLE
& GLASS

Brindle & Glass
An imprint of TouchWood Editions
Brindleandglass.com

The information in this book is true and complete to the best of the author's knowledge. Care has been taken to trace the ownership of copyright material used in this book. The author and the publisher welcome any information enabling them to rectify any references or credit in subsequent editions.

Design by Pete Kohut

Cover images: Top row: Belcourt family collection. Bottom: Pgiam, istockphoto.com
Interior photos: All photos are from the Belcourt family collection,
except those indicated.
Belcourt family tree created by: jellyfish design, jellyfishdesign.com

LIBRARY AND ARCHIVES CANADA CATALOGUING IN PUBLICATION
Belcourt, Herb, 1931–, author
Walking in the woods : a Métis memoir / Herb Belcourt.

Reprinted with revised preface.
Issued in print and electronic formats.
ISBN 978-1-927366-71-4 (softcover)

1. Belcourt, Herb, 1931–. 2. Métis—Biography. 3. Canada, Western—
Biography. 4. Autobiographies. I. Title.

FC109.1.B44A3 2017   971.2'004970092   C2017-903036-1

We acknowledge the financial support of the Government of Canada through the Canada Book Fund and the Canada Council for the Arts, and of the Province of British Columbia through the British Columbia Arts Council and the Book Publishing Tax Credit.

The interior pages of this book have been printed on 100% post-consumer recycled paper, processed chlorine free, and printed with vegetable-based inks.

PRINTED IN CANADA AT FRIESENS

17 18 19 20 21   5 4 3 2 1

To my sister, Viola,
with my admiration for your strength, courage,
and patience through a challenging illness.

PUBLISHER'S NOTE

On July 5, 2017, Herb Belcourt passed away peacefully at his home, surrounded by his loved ones, just a month before this new edition of his book went to press. We will remember Herb as a kind and generous man with an incredible way of connecting with people.

CONTENTS

* * *

Unveiling the plaque at the newly named Herb Belcourt Park.

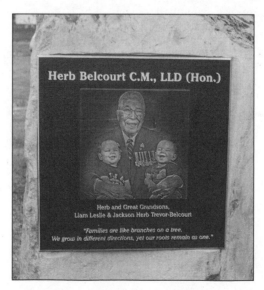

Herb Belcourt C.M., LLD (Hon.)

Herb and Great Grandsons,
Liam Leslie & Jackson Herb Trevor-Belcourt

*"Families are like branches on a tree.
We grow in different directions, yet our roots remain as one."*

Preface to the 2017 Edition

AFTER WALKING IN THE WOODS in 2006, I lingered to let my roots deepen. Our family still owns a lot of land at Lac Ste. Anne. I traced places I had heard about, among them my birthplace where the original cabin (long gone) was so poorly insulated boiling water froze in the kettle overnight. I reacquainted myself with the area I had left behind, talking with friends and family about the years I had missed. The result was a Belcourt family reunion—held on my cousin Bob's land in August 2007—that brought together relatives from across the country to celebrate 225 years of one of Alberta's oldest families. It was a wonderful reunion.

We rented a tent that held a thousand people. Family jumped in and helped. We used laptops to gather important information: everyone's names, where they came from, and what they were doing. A person doesn't realize how many relatives they actually have until they show up for a celebration like this and camp out across the land.

They came from BC, Saskatchewan, Ontario, southern Alberta, Peace River, Grand Prairie, Fort McMurray, Marlboro, and from around Lac Ste. Anne itself, of course—Darwell and Wabamun. Some brought guitars and fiddles and we danced and sang.

I felt so much at home here that in 2009 I bought a cabin on the lake in Val Quentin, a short drive from the Métis settlements and mission where the annual pilgrimage is held. Sitting on the porch and watching herons, loons, and plovers feeding on the lake was a pleasure. Seeing geese trustingly move goslings from the water and sit them under their wings on my grass was a joy. Muskrats would swim by in the early hours just after the sun rose. I relished those still, peaceful moments with nature.

Since writing *Walking in the Woods* ten years ago, I still get calls from people asking if they can get another book from me, as they want to give it to a friend or relative as a gift. Others stop to tell me how much they enjoyed reading it or how they couldn't put it down. Since writing it, a lot of changes have happened. My elder son, David, died shortly after it was published. Then I lost three sisters and three brothers. I am so glad their stories will continue to be shared in this book.

On a more positive note: my granddaughter Amethyst, who came with me on my journey through the woods when she was only eleven, brought into the world on March 20, 2016 two beautiful identical boys, Liam and Jackson—my great-grandsons. They bring me so much joy.

For the past ten years, I have remained active in many of the same organizations, but I also added a few. In 2008 I became a member of the University of Alberta Gathering Place, and in 2010 Chair of the Native

Counselling Homelessness Project while continuing as a board member for Native Counselling Services of Alberta until 2012. I became Vice Chair of Métis Nation Rupertsland Institute Board of Governors in 2010, then acted as Interim Chair 2011–2013 and again in 2014. I was a board member on Grant MacEwan's Faculty of Business from 2010 until 2013. My term on the RCMP Commanding Officer's Aboriginal Elders Advisory Committee "K" Division ended in 2013, but they gave me an honorary ambassador position instead; after three years on the board of Amiskwaciy Cultural Society I was made an honorary member in 2016.

But the majority of my time by far has been devoted to the Belcourt Brosseau Métis Awards (BBMA) that Georges Brosseau, Orval Belcourt, and I established after we liquidated Canative Housing.

Each year, at a dinner, we honour the BBMA students by highlighting their successes and our culture. In September 2016, we celebrated our fifteenth anniversary. Over one hundred alumni opened our ceremony carrying torches into the darkened room. These former recipients of our awards, who had graduated in many disciplines to become successful in their chosen fields, acted as an inspiration to those students about to take part in their own sash ceremony initiated by Elder Marge Friedel and Theresa Majeran in 2006. Their entry brought tears to many eyes.

Over this past year I have been in emergency several times, and on two separate occasions I met two nurses who had received awards from our BBMA fund. They gave me such huge hugs. One brought flowers to my bedside. At a funeral recently, the niece of the deceased hugged me, saying she, too, through BBMA had been able to graduate as a social worker and was giving back to Aboriginal people. On another occasion, while watching a parade at Alberta Beach, I was unexpectedly hugged from behind by a woman studying education on the strength of her BBMA award. Having so many loving hugs is the sweetest reward I could receive. It tells me that all these years have been worthwhile and that our work has changed people's lives for the better. Recipients and their families continue in the spirit of family and give back, making donations to our fund, allowing it to grow and flourish. I am so proud of them.

I have been honoured to receive many awards. In 2010 I was made a member of the Order of Canada. In 2011 I received the Rotary Club of Sherwood Park's Integrity Award, followed by the Queen's Diamond Jubilee Medal in 2012. Although NorQuest College had named their auditorium after me earlier, the room was removed during major renovations, so instead the Dr. Herb Belcourt Boardroom was named in my honour in 2014. That same year NorQuest awarded me an Honorary Diploma, and a few months later NAIT awarded me the Senator Thelma Chalifoux Award.

On January 31, 2017, I received the Lifetime Achievement Award from the Canadian Council for Aboriginal Business Hall of Fame in Toronto. This same year, on May 3, Alberta inducted me into the Junior Achievement Business Hall of Fame, and on June 12, 2017, on behalf of the Salute to Excellence Council, Georges, Orval, and I had our portraits installed in the City of Edmonton's Community Service Hall of Fame.

But probably the highlight of all these honours

occurred on May 10 when Strathcona County and friends from our community, along with RCMP and Edmonton police, unveiled a plaque dedicated to me in the newly named Herb Belcourt Park. The plaque fixed to a huge stone is of me with my twin great-grandsons Liam and Jackson. Such a proud moment.

Although I greatly appreciate these acknowledgements, the most inspiring gifts are letters from BBMA students telling me of their journeys and how their lives have changed for the better. At some stage I want to compile these into a book to inspire others to follow their dreams and pursue their goals. Everything is possible. You just have to believe in yourself and say, "I can!"

And I still have more dreams to pursue. One particularly dear to my heart is to establish a healing centre for women with addictions. Why women? Throughout my life I have had the most success in helping women. They are the hub of the family, child-bearers, educators, the ones who shape young lives. They are the role models for future generations. And they are motivated to make life better. I watched women make enormous strides at Canative's Life Skills program, and I see more women through BBMA in further education becoming successful. The feminine, symbolized by the circle, is an important part of Aboriginal society. After all, the Creator traditionally is both male and female. How could it be otherwise?

At a practical level, any healing centre must offer ongoing support. The healing centre I envision would focus on those aspects of life that we associate with the feminine—creativity—so I visualize a program that I have already named *Healing Waters*, which includes activities to encourage healthy nurturing of self and others. Research shows that people heal better in "green" (nature) surroundings, but even better in "blue" environments that include water (also linked at a spiritual level with emotions), so location is important, away from urban areas, in natural surroundings, close to water, in the arms of Mother Nature. I imagine that some of the land at Métis Crossing at Smokey Lake overlooking the North Saskatchewan river may be a perfect place.

But time is slipping through my fingers. Diagnosed recently with stage four cancer, I know my time is limited. It just means I have to move faster to get things done. I have always said we cannot do things alone. So maybe if I just sow some seeds others will water them and see them to fruition. That is the Aboriginal way, working together in cooperation. I have great faith this will happen.

Herb Belcourt

Herb Belcourt
2017

Foreword to the 2006 Edition

I HAVE KNOWN HERB BELCOURT—AT FIRST by reputation, and later as a colleague and friend—for most of my life. I hope his moving story will open a window on the independence, energy, and generosity of the Métis people of western Canada.

How would I describe him? He is a hard-working man, devoted to his wife and family, and very successful in business. He loves to talk about his grandchildren. He is also a proud Métis and a generous supporter of the Métis people. I can tell you two stories that will demonstrate the distance this man will go to create opportunities for young people, and to honour our elders and our Métis heritage.

I became acquainted with Herb when I first began to work for the Métis Nation of Alberta in 1991. He was on the board of Apeetogosan (Métis) Development Inc., our financial lending institution, and I was the financial officer for the Métis Nation. We began a working relationship that grew stronger after I was elected the president of the Métis Nation of Alberta in 1996.

Herb left school early in his life, as people often did in his generation. He has always talked about the importance of education for our people: having the opportunity not only to go to school, but also to pursue a meaningful job, a vocation or profession, a chosen career that will satisfy a person throughout life. When Herb and his colleagues, Georges Brosseau and Orval Belcourt, decided to fund the Belcourt Brosseau Métis Awards, he came to ask for my support. "It will take all of us to move this forward," he said. I was happy to help.

Few Canadians are aware that Métis students do not have the educational opportunities of other Aboriginal people for tuition funding. We have to find our own way to raise the money. In a short time, the Belcourt Brosseau Métis Awards program has grown to a fourteen million dollar scholarship fund for Métis post-secondary students. It has been so beneficial. We have students who come to us and say: "I couldn't have gone on to post-secondary studies without this award. It feels so good to know that I can put this plan forward, and someone is looking out for me, so I can go ahead and finish school. Someone cares about who I want to be and where I want to go in life." Someone certainly cares. The Belcourt Brosseau partnership has also contributed large endowments to many of Alberta's fine post-secondary institutions. These benefactors are creating a legacy of learning that will continue for a long, long time to come.

Herb's dream is that the federal and provincial governments, as well as Alberta industries and individual citizens, will match the dollars in the scholarship fund to increase opportunities for Métis students across western Canada. I would like to see his dream fulfilled, and I hope this book will be a starting place for that campaign.

Most of us recognize that a true education continues throughout life, outside the classrooms in colleges and universities. I have always been passionate about the idea of cultural education—for the Métis people, so that they will continue to honour their culture, language, and history, and for their neighbours in the community, who might not know more about the Métis story than the historic names of Louis Riel or Gabriel Dumont, Red River and Batoche.

The Métis people of Alberta—our leaders, our elders, and our members across the province—have talked for a long time about the need for a cultural education centre. We wanted a place where we could meet, a place where we could celebrate our history and traditions, a place we could call home together. We searched for opportunities for years, but did not find any that we could pursue. In 1998, we began to talk to the provincial government about the possibility, and with their help, we completed the Millennium Voyage research project. Researchers identified sixty-three gathering places and communities across Alberta where Métis people had resided over the centuries.

Suddenly, a perfect opportunity came along. A farm family, originally from Ontario and of German background, came to the Métis Nation of Alberta in 1998 with an offer to sell 512 acres near the North Saskatchewan River, about one hour east of Edmonton. This land had been in the possession of Métis people throughout the generations until 1975, when the Ontario family purchased it. When the husband passed away, his wife looked at it and said: "This land needs to go back to the Métis." She offered it to us at a set price, and told us: "I believe it should be in your hands."

We badly wanted to buy the land, but we did not have the money. The price was six hundred thousand dollars. We knew there was no way we could purchase the property, make payments, and develop it, even though we had strengthened our relationships with our banker and the government. We had people who believed in us. We asked the banker to hold the land for us, and promised that we would find a way to pay the interest for six months. After that, we convinced the bank we needed a little more time! I went to Herb Belcourt to ask for help. "I know you believe in education," I said. "Cultural education, for our people and for the rest of the public in Alberta, is important, too." He listened to me, and asked many questions. We had a meeting with the three gentlemen—Herb, Georges, and Orval—and presented our plans. We tried very, very hard to convince them that this could be a good thing. They promised that they would buy the land if we could get development funding from the province, on the condition that the land would always remain a Métis cultural centre to educate our people. We applied for a one-million-dollar Alberta centennial grant, and we worked very hard to get it. I think Herb and I were the happiest people alive when we got the call that we had been successful.

Métis Crossing opened in the summer of 2005 in its first phase, to give the public a preview, and we already have a small staff on site to welcome a limited number of visitors. We are planning our grand opening in 2008. The federal government has identified the larger area—encompassing the Victoria Mission and Métis Crossing—as a national historic site. We hope thousands of Canadians will celebrate our heritage with us at Métis Crossing in the years to come.

I LIVE IN the Métis homeland, and like Herb Belcourt, I can trace my family lineage to the first people who lived in the vast territory that is now western Canada. We are the proud descendants of the indigenous women of our homeland, and the French- or English-speaking men who travelled west as voyageurs and fur traders in the eighteenth and nineteenth centuries, before Canada became a nation. Our ancestors had children and grand-children who married other Métis westerners and created a distinctive way of life as one of Canada's founding Aboriginal peoples. The Belcourt family lived for gener-ations around Lac Ste. Anne, a historic Métis community just northwest of present-day Edmonton, and one of a number of distinct Métis communities along the water-ways of northwestern Canada.

I want all Canadians, and diverse people around the world, to know more about our rich history and culture, and to understand our significant place among the world's Aboriginal peoples. We had to fight hard for recognition—in the famous historic confrontations of 1870 and 1885, and also through the negotiations and court challenges of the twentieth century. In 1982, Canada recognized the Métis as Aboriginal people in an explicit reference in the Constitution. At the time, our leaders, and all of us, thought this constitutional recog-nition would change the world for us. We thought that Canada would recognize us, finally, as equals among the other Aboriginal peoples of Canada: the First Nations and the Inuit. That didn't happen. Not a lot changed.

It took many years, and expensive court battles, before the Supreme Court of Canada affirmed in 2003 that we do have Aboriginal rights that are equal to the enduring rights of other Aboriginal peoples. In a case involving two Métis hunters, Steve and Roddy Powley, charged for hunting without a licence, the Supreme Court of Canada ruled that the Métis have an Aboriginal right to harvest from the land, protected by the Constitution. Immediately after the Powley decision, we came home to negotiate the Interim Métis Harvesting Agreement with the province of Alberta. There have been a few problems, but I believe we have that fundamental recognition in Alberta. That certainly hasn't been the case for the Métis in all provinces. The Powley decision is not just about hunting. It is about the recognition of our legal rights, and our identity as Métis people.

So who are we today? The Métis National Council developed a definition of the Métis people in 2002 based on an individual's genealogy, and personal and community identity. We define our historic homeland, roughly, as the three Prairie provinces of Alberta, Manitoba, and Saskatchewan; portions of northwestern Ontario, British Columbia, and the Northwest Territories; as well as some northern states in the United States, such as North Dakota and Montana. By this definition, we estimate there are 400,000 citizens of the Métis Nation in Canada, although not all westerners are aware of their Métis family lineage. In the 2001 federal census, almost 263,000 people west of Ontario chose to identify themselves as Métis. Today, two-thirds of the Métis live in cities and towns..

Here in Alberta, more than 66,000 people identified themselves as Métis in the last census; about 34,000 have come forward voluntarily to register with the Métis Nation of Alberta. Of the sixty-three communities in the province that can claim a distinct and enduring Métis heritage, Lac Ste. Anne holds a special place in our history.

Herb Belcourt's story begins as a search for his Métis family roots on the land near Lac Ste. Anne. It is a different kind of pilgrimage to this historic gathering place, a search for one man's personal history, ideas, and values, and one family's identity. I agree with Herb that Métis land issues are confusing to the Canadian public and to the Métis people themselves. The Canadian government signed treaties with the First Nations of the West in the nineteenth century, but could not extinguish the Aboriginal title of the Métis on the Prairies through the distribution of scrip—a kind of coupon that could be redeemed in land. The federal government distributed scrip in the Edmonton area in the summers of 1885 and 1886. This highly unsuccessful system resulted in huge transfers of public property to Canadian scrip speculators, and widespread irregularities. Many Métis families found themselves without the land that they had considered their own for centuries. Somehow, they sustained communities and preserved traditions. Strong, early leaders—Joseph Dion, Malcolm Norris, Jim Brady, Adrian Hope, and many others—founded l'Association des Métis d'Alberta et des Territoires du Nord-ouest in 1932, which they reorganized and renamed the Métis Association of Alberta in 1940.

Alberta is unusual in Canada in that it has an independent Métis land base of eight settlements, established under Alberta legislation in the 1930s. However, we have not yet resolved all difficult land issues. Between the Métis and First Nations, there remain differences of opinion about land, and legal rights and how we should interpret them. Our communities overlap sometimes, and our families have intermarried. In some places—Cadotte Lake near Peace River is a good example—we are finding that First Nations members have community services and facilities that are not available to Métis neighbours, who are often relatives.

The government of Canada has not recognized all of our historic claims as Aboriginal people. We will confront those battles somewhere down the line. Canadians need to know we are not asking for handouts. We are asking for what we rightly believe is ours. We have our struggles and challenges, but we also have the drive to make things change, and the ability to work hard to achieve our goals. By telling his story, with strength and humour, Herb Belcourt is passing on the values of his community to a new generation.

I think the Métis are a very patient people, a very generous people, a very hard-working people—and our rewards will come.

Audrey Poitras,
President of the Métis Nation of Alberta
June 2006

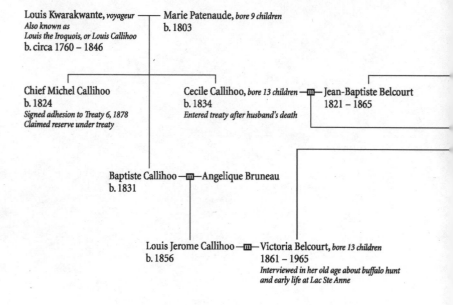

Louis Kwarakwante, *voyageur* ——— Marie Patenaude, *bore 9 children*
Also known as b. 1803
Louis the Iroquois, or Louis Callihoo
b. circa 1760 – 1846

Chief Michel Callihoo Cecile Callihoo, *bore 13 children* —ⅿ— Jean-Baptiste Belcourt
b. 1824 b. 1834 1821 – 1865
Signed adhesion to Treaty 6, 1878 *Entered treaty after husband's death*
Claimed reserve under treaty

Baptiste Callihoo —ⅿ—Angelique Bruneau
b. 1831

Louis Jerome Callihoo —ⅿ— Victoria Belcourt, *bore 13 children*
b. 1856 1861 – 1965
Interviewed in her old age about buffalo hunt
and early life at Lac Ste Anne

THE BELCOURTS: A FAMILY TREE

A friendship between two voyageurs, Joseph Belcourt and Louise Kwarakwante, in the early 1800s, led to a strong connection between the two large families through marriages in subsequent generations. Some descendants claimed treaty status under Treaty 6 while others applied for Metis scrip at Lac Ste. Anne and St. Albert after 1885. This is a simplified chart of much larger families. Thousands of descendants live in the Edmonton area today.

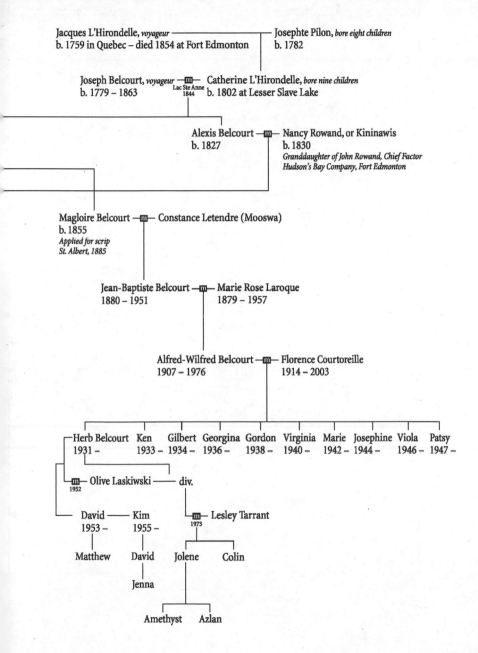

Jacques L'Hirondelle, *voyageur*
b. 1759 in Quebec – died 1854 at Fort Edmonton
┬ Josephte Pilon, *bore eight children*
b. 1782

Joseph Belcourt, *voyageur* —Ⓜ— Catherine L'Hirondelle, *bore nine children*
b. 1779 – 1863 *Lac Ste Anne 1844* b. 1802 at Lesser Slave Lake

Alexis Belcourt —Ⓜ— Nancy Rowand, or Kininawis
b. 1827 b. 1830
*Granddaughter of John Rowand, Chief Factor
Hudson's Bay Company, Fort Edmonton*

Magloire Belcourt —Ⓜ— Constance Letendre (Mooswa)
b. 1855
*Applied for scrip
St. Albert, 1885*

Jean-Baptiste Belcourt —Ⓜ— Marie Rose Laroque
1880 – 1951 1879 – 1957

Alfred-Wilfred Belcourt —Ⓜ— Florence Courtoreille
1907 – 1976 1914 – 2003

Herb Belcourt Ken Gilbert Georgina Gordon Virginia Marie Josephine Viola Patsy
1931 – 1933 – 1934 – 1936 – 1938 – 1940 – 1942 – 1944 – 1946 – 1947 –

—Ⓜ— Olive Laskiwski —— div.
1952

David —— Kim —Ⓜ— Lesley Tarrant
1953 – 1955 – *1973*

Matthew David Jolene Colin

Jenna

Amethyst Azlan

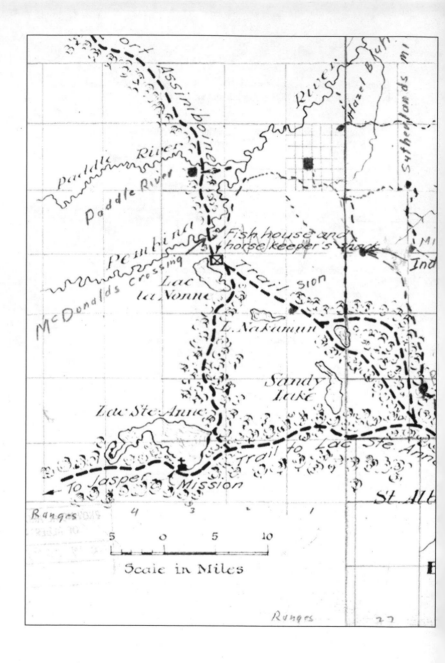

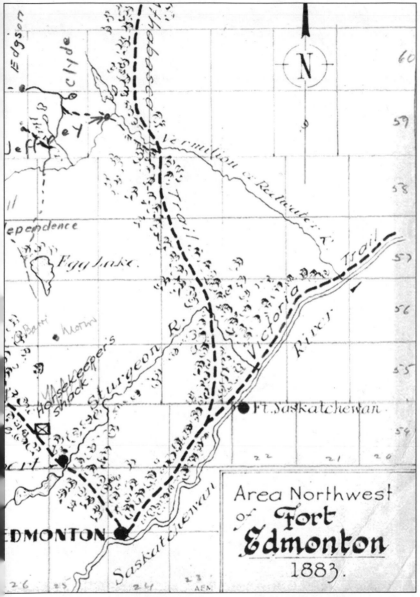

The trail from Fort Edmonton to Lac Ste. Anne, 1883.

Exploring the Woods

I USED TO SAY WHEN I was young that I never wanted to be as poor as my mum and dad. I didn't realize at that time that we were rich. We had everything we needed at Lac Ste. Anne, although I did not understand that for a long time. As the oldest boy in a family of ten children, I left home at the age of fifteen with a one-way bus ticket to my first job and a life of my own. Except for short visits to see my family, I never lived in Lac Ste. Anne again.

I return more often these days. The place means more to me now that I am an older man. I am looking for a trail through the woods, a path I have lost, and that is where I want to begin this story.

Last Saturday I drove out to the lake with my wife, Lesley, and our grandchildren, Amethyst and Azlan. I told them I wanted to find an old wagon trail on the land that had once belonged to the Belcourt family. I was hoping the old fencelines would still be in place, and I could find the farm where we had lived when I was a child. Lesley and I approach everything in life as a team, and she is as interested in this search as I am. Our grandchildren, who we are raising, are willing to go on any road trip as long as they can bring along their dog, Snuggles, who is quite an entertainer. We left home in the early morning. It was one of those perfect Alberta days in the first part of summer: blue skies with no clouds, and bright sunshine all the way. We live in Sherwood Park, a large community of fifty-five thousand people just beyond Edmonton's eastern city limits, our home for thirty years. We drove straight west across the middle of Edmonton, and then followed the highway west and north to reach the little community where I was born. The trip takes about an hour.

We stopped first at our trailer at Alberta Beach, a summer village on Lac Ste. Anne. Lesley and the kids walked to the water to give the dog some exercise. Amethyst ran along the side of the road with Snuggles. Azlan was the first to notice the red-winged blackbirds in the marsh. I talked to our weekend neighbours for a while and joined my family for a snack at the café. I have been thinking about buying land around here, off and on, looking around, but the area is growing quickly with new developments for city people. Today small cabins and new homes take up most of the shoreline around the lake, except for the Alexis reserve and the remaining property still owned by orders of the Roman Catholic Church. Property prices are rising quickly around here. I haven't made a decision. How relaxing will this place be in the future, and what will it look like? I am not sure.

When the kids finished their pizza, we climbed back

into the car, and followed the old road around the s
shore of the lake to the old community of Lac Ste. A

The Lac Ste. Anne Trail used to be the main ruutc
between Fort Edmonton and Jasper, connected to the
Fort Assiniboine Trail. Today a paved highway follows
the south shore of the lake, twisting and turning, from
Alberta Beach to Lac St. Anne to Darwell and on to the
west. The route of the old, historic trail criss-crosses
the paved road, veering off by a few kilometres in some
places, and crossing back again. I think it would be good
to take tourists on a walk along the old trail, if the exact
route could be identified. That isn't easy.

I looked out the car window at the house trailers
and a new development scraping the land. This entire
area will soon fill up with big houses, house trailers, city
people and their trailers. I am worried that the crowding
of people will spoil the area. It would be a different story
if the new people built a community to honour the way
people once lived, but the way they are doing it now,
sometimes it looks tacky. The Letendres lived along this
stretch of the road. Old Billy Letendre and the others.
I remembered the old, log houses on this road, and the
narrow lanes that led through the trees to other families.
The houses were small, whitewashed, and surrounded by
shady poplar trees and rolling pasture. The lake sparkled
behind them.

We turned into the yard of my cousin, Bob Belcourt,
who still keeps a place here, although his permanent
home is south of here. We found him cutting firewood
with a chainsaw. "Take a look around," he said, when he
saw us. Bob's grandfather, William John Belcourt, and
my grandfather, Jean-Baptiste Belcourt, were brothers.

Old W.J. Belcourt built a log house on this land beside the old mission church more than a century ago. By some kind of miracle, it is still standing. It is one of the only log houses still here to remind me of the way Lac Ste. Anne used to be. The roof has collapsed, but the walls are strong.

We walked around the old log house for a long time. I put my hand against the old beams, remembering. Lesley took photographs. The kids played with a small country mutt that had come over to inspect Snuggles. When I looked at their bare feet, and I touched the old logs on the house, it brought me back to the days when I was a kid. I looked through the wide cracks between the logs, and imagined the good times we shared in rooms just like that one. We had a happy family: aunts, uncles, and neighbours, mostly related. There was always laughter around us. We had all the food we needed. There was no liquor at any of our parties. When we had company, there would be storytelling, fiddle music, a dance, a jig. I don't remember ever being without clothes, or anything I really needed. We had a whole support system. Neighbours helped one another. Everyone built a barn, a log barn for Mum and Dad, and all the neighbours came along and helped. If someone killed a moose, all the families shared it. Whenever we butchered a hog, we made blood sausages and shared them with everyone. We had lots of eggs and vegetables. Our cellar was always full. We picked blueberries and gooseberries, and my mother preserved all the wild berries. Looking back now, I can say again that we were rich.

In the winter, sleighs would come down this road, with the bells on their horses, all coming together to the Catholic Church beside my uncle's house. I was an altar boy in that church. It is funny what kids notice and remember. My father told me he worked for the priests when he was young, diverting a creek, and later the priests told the local people that everything west of the creek belonged to the church. The Grey Nuns own a lot of this land now, and we stopped to look at the property beyond the gate. Somehow the nuns got all of this land around the mission, all through here; some of it used to be Belcourt land. Uncle Alex bought the fish from the fishermen around here, too; he was a fish buyer the way my father was a fur buyer. It is a shame the church has so much of this land today, but maybe in another way, it was a method of preserving it. I think the whole area should be a historic site, to preserve it forever from too much development.

We drove over to park in the churchyard. Lesley and I walked into the cemetery. I remembered the funerals when I was a kid, and I pointed to the place where the people tied their horses, and another path where the men had carried the coffins from the church to the graveyard. A stone marker lists the first Métis and Cree-Iroquois families in the district: Callihoo, Wanyandi, Brazeau, Breland, Auger, Collin, Dumont, Savard, Kalliou, Gaucher, Hamelin, Gruyere, Asines, Dumont. These are the families of the early fur trade in Alberta, who settled here when they worked for the North West Company and the Hudson's Bay Company at Fort Edmonton, and who later worked for themselves as trappers, fur traders, and farmers. Generations of Belcourts were buried in this small cemetery. Lesley and I walked slowly, reading markers with birthdates in the early and mid-1800s.

I found the grave of my grandfather, Jean-Baptiste Belcourt, 1880–1951, and my grandmother, Marie Rose Laroque Belcourt, buried beside him beneath a simple wooden cross, carved with the word "Rose." Old W.J. Belcourt, the man who built the log house, is buried nearby; he was born in 1884. So many Métis families in Alberta, and across western Canada, can trace their roots to this community. The family stones here carry their names: the L'Hirondelle family, the Karakonti family, the Gray, Loyer, Courtreille, Tourangeau, Letendre, Courtipatte, and Laderoute families.

We waited for Azlan, who was playing with a Frisbee not too far away. We started to drive again, and soon passed the old Protestant cemetery. I don't think I was ever there once. I remember some bad feelings in those days. Once a Protestant got very sick, and needed to go quickly to the hospital. Our priest was the only one in the community at the time with a car. He wouldn't drive the Protestant to the hospital. There was a lot of bitterness about that. Although Lac Ste. Anne started out as a Métis community, and continued to be one over the century, English-speaking Protestant farmers also settled around here in the late 1800s and early 1900s. Everyone had to learn to live together.

On the same road, we passed the house where the medicine woman had lived. Keeskatas, we called her. She was a Letendre. We followed the old road to a T-intersection, then turned south until we reached a small lane, heading west. This, I think, was part of the old Lac Ste. Anne Trail, too. Think of it. This little lane was once the main road between Fort Edmonton and the Pacific coast. I could almost see the early people riding wagons here. I told the kids that I remembered riding a horse here, too, when I was their age.

"Do you wish you could still do it, Grandpa?" Amethyst asked. We continued to drive the car along two mud tracks between tall poplar trees, swerving around mudholes, and bumping along. Lesley warned me that we would probably get stuck if we continued. A minute later, as she predicted, we reached a deep mud-hole, and I had to turn the car around to find another way to our destination.

Soon we were driving past the corner of land where the old Beaudry School used to be. Fish Billy lived around here. Nancy Belcourt's land was here beside the railroad tracks. Joe Williams, a Black man, lived near the corner.

"Grandpa," said Amethyst from the back seat. "Can I ask you one question? Where are we going?"

I told her I was looking for a corner of land where I grew up with my parents and brothers and sisters, and the farm nearby where my grandparents had built their log home many years earlier. "It was all Belcourt land," I said.

"Maybe old ghosts haunt this place," said Azlan.

The land, the farms, the owners—all have changed in the sixty years since I lived here as a boy. It wasn't easy for me to find the road allowance, the old fencelines, or any recognized boundaries of my family's land. I kept searching for the right lane. At last I turned into a farm driveway, and stopped beside a pickup truck in the yard. A little girl waved to us, and her mother appeared behind her to greet the visitors, along with two friendly dogs. The Stokes family live here now, raising sheep and cattle. They're planning to build a big house on the property. "Was there an old log house here?" I asked. "Or a trail in the woods back there?" The woman told me she hadn't seen anything like that, but we were welcome to look. She unlocked two ranch gates, and warned us about the new bull who might not take kindly to visitors. She left us alone to explore, but the family's two dogs decided to keep us company, as a warning signal to the coyotes in the woods. We climbed to the top of a hill, and looked back at the ranch and the surrounding woods of birch and poplar. We could see horses in the distance. Amethyst and Azlan ran off ahead of us, with the dogs beside them, and circled to meet us.

We walked across this beautiful land for several hours. Was this the right place? I needed to know, but nothing could help me be sure. Lesley and I had explored this area alone once before, about thirty years ago, but we had approached it from a different direction. This time it was more confusing. I had visualized the old trail, the road and the wagon tracks, hoping they would help me identify the land. I couldn't find these clues. I was frustrated, at first, because the land had once been so familiar to me. We found old, rusting farm equipment on the hill—a rake and the box of an old winter sleigh, its steel runners buried in the grass and dirt. I wondered if they could have once belonged to my grandparents. Did I ride on that sleigh?

We entered the woods and started to climb up a wide trail. I remembered my own dog, pulling me to school through the woods on a smaller sleigh. I wish I had come back here to appreciate nature on this land a little sooner. I think all of us need to do that. These woods were full of berries, small animals, birds—full of life. It was just like a park here, with big trees. When I was much younger, after my father sold the family land and moved to the city, an uncle had offered to sell a large piece of family property to me for sixteen hundred dollars. I didn't have that money then, and maybe I didn't want the land then, either.

I kept thinking about what I would have done with that land, the possibility of it, as I walked among the trees. It is really too bad that a person waits until he gets older to do something important, and then thinks: I wish I'd done this sooner. I wish I had 160 acres somewhere: not farmland, just bush, and a lovely cabin there, not a big place, two rooms in it with a verandah. I would go there to relax and think, to walk through the bush, listen to the birds, see the animals. I would like to have some water nearby for the ducks, the birds. I suppose that is a dream now.

I don't usually like walking so much. I have trouble with my hips and legs, so I had to stop to rest more often than I would have liked. I leaned against a tree to give me energy. The kids came back to show us rocks that they had found. Soon we were all leaning against trees, looking up through the leaves at the blue sky.

"If you were lost, and you wanted to know which way was north, what would you do?" I asked Amethyst. She looked at me, waiting for an answer. "The tree will give you a hint," Lesley said. We showed her the moss that was growing on the north side of the tree. Amethyst and Azlan started running again, the dogs at their heels. When we finally turned around, as the sun was going down, Amethyst said: "This is the best day I've had for two years." She put two rocks in the trunk of the car. I knew what she meant. It felt good to be on this land. Very, very good.

We tried to think of a title for this book as we drove along the road. Azlan had the first suggestion.

"You should call it *The Magic Lake*," he said.

Amethyst had her own ideas. "*The Loving Belcourt Family*," she said. "*The Belcourt Past*."

Her brother is eight years old, and he doesn't let his ten-year-old sister get the last word.

"What about *The Belcourt Crystal Clear Lake*?"

I appreciated their suggestions, but I kept returning in my thoughts to my search in the woods that day. It was a day when I realized, again, how much Lac Ste. Anne means to me, and to the Métis people in our part of Canada. This walk seemed like a good way to begin my book.

Like many older men, I like to tell stories when I meet my friends at the coffee shop in the morning. Many people have encouraged me to write a book. The more I thought about the idea, the more I felt deep down in my gut that I wanted to do it. The feeling intensified last year when I became seriously ill. I had what I thought was a heart attack. It turned out to be a heart condition called bradycardia, where my heart slowed down. I had three or four attacks at home, one in the ambulance, and one on the metal slab at the University of Alberta Hospital. I was in intensive care for five days, I believe it was, and I darn near died. They put an external pacemaker into me, and then later another pacemaker. I wasn't feeling well, and I kept going back and forth to emergency for some time. In June 2005, I learned I had prostate cancer, a very aggressive cancer, and my doctors were afraid at first that the cancer was in my bones, too. I had to take forty days of radiation treatments, five days a week, and the last ten days were so awful I did not know if I could continue. My last radiation day was January 13, 2006.

I remember thinking then that I had to write everything down, that I would not be like my father, who did not write anything before he died, although he knew so much about the fur business in Alberta. That knowledge went with him. I want to leave something behind to assist young people, particularly young Native people, because it is their world coming up. Mine is finished.

The only thing I can leave behind is a little knowledge I have learned along the way. That, and some encouragement.

What would they think if they met me? Maybe they would see a retired businessman, an older person who might become a friend. I am seventy-five years old, a tall man, about six foot one, and people always notice the size of my hands when I shake hands with them. They grab my hand and say, "Let me get a hold of this properly." When I was young, my nickname was *Mahkicihciy*, which means big hands. I am a friendly person. I hope that everyone's first impression of me is my friendliness. I like to speak with a bit of humour. I don't usually tell people what they want to hear, and I suppose that's why I've never won as a candidate in politics, but I try to be diplomatic.

I recently heard that I am winning my fight with cancer, so I am grateful for this extra time in my life. What will I do with it? I always think about what I am going to do in the future. I am not one to make a decision immediately. I must think about it, plan down the road, and consider how it should turn out. I ask myself questions all the time. Where do you want to go? Where do you want to be at a certain time? I have always looked ahead. Lately, I have been learning to look back at my life, to consider what it has taught me. I walk slowly, because I do a lot of thinking when I walk slowly.

I do not claim to be a professional writer. For the past few months, I have been sitting in my den at home, thinking over experiences and questions, and telling my story into a tape recorder for hours at a time. This project has been a family effort. I have asked my nine brothers and sisters to help me, and they have spoken into the same tape recorder, and found photographs and documents for this book, too. Lesley typed each one of our transcripts, making suggestions and asking more questions. She encouraged me to say everything that was on my mind and in my heart, everything I consider valuable. If I have made errors in this book, or misinterpreted people or events, I am truly sorry. I have told this story as honestly as I could, from my own perspective, the way I remember it. The story begins, and ends, at Lac Ste. Anne.

CHAPTER ONE

Pilgrimage to Lac Ste. Anne

LAC STE. ANNE HAS ALWAYS been considered a holy place by the Native people, a lake with healing powers. They called it Spirit Lake, or God's Lake, in their languages, but the priests of the Catholic Church renamed it Ste. Anne, after Jesus' grandmother. I believe the Church started the Lac Ste. Anne pilgrimage as it is known today. There were a certain number of days for the white people and for the Native people, so they had separate pilgrimages. That tradition carries on today. The pilgrimage has survived from one July to the next for 117 years.

As a boy, I recall people coming to Lac Ste. Anne for the pilgrimage in horse-drawn buggies, with tents tied behind, and I remember covered wagons full of children. People came from all over the province. Some travelled for a week. They came as families, with their dogs following behind. I remember seeing a wagon with the family's cow tied behind it. Some came in old trucks that looked like cattle trucks, with thirty or forty people

An unidentified family camp at the Lac Ste. Anne
pilgrimage in the early years of the gathering.
PHOTO OB8575N APPEARS COURTESY OF THE MISSIONARY OBLATES,
GRANDIN COLLECTION, PROVINCIAL ARCHIVES OF ALBERTA

in the back. They all seemed so happy, laughing, seeing
their old friends. It was a spiritual journey, in one way,
but it was also a big social get-together where people
could meet their old friends and relatives. They came
by the hundreds. They would camp in their tents all
around the church. Today people arrive with campers
and motorhomes, but they come to Lac Ste. Anne for the
same reasons as I witnessed in my childhood.

Lac Ste. Anne came alive during the pilgrimage. It
appeared to me as if the whole family had come home.
The church set up a shed where people could buy
rosaries and holy water from the lake. Some people
set up tables and sold their old clothes. Once they had
reached the lake, the people prayed, and walked around
the shrines in the hundreds. They waded into the lake.
Some were crippled, and very sick. I remember one
woman in a wheelchair. Her family pushed her into the
lake, and after praying awhile with people around her,

she got up from the wheelchair and walked out of the water. I was astonished.

The Native people of western Canada—the Métis and the First Nations alike—love Lac Ste. Anne for many reasons. It has been a gathering place for Aboriginal people for thousands of years. In 1994, archaeologists found stone remainders of an arrowhead or knife that they dated between five thousand and six thousand years old. The Nakoda people, once known as the Stoneys or Assiniboines, continue to live on the Alexis reserve on the north shore. They call the lake *Wakãmne* in their language. The Cree called it *Manito Sakahigan*. Métis families lived along the south shore 160 years ago, perhaps longer, back in the days when they were buffalo hunters, voyageurs, freighters, and fish suppliers on contract to supply the Hudson's Bay Company at Fort Edmonton. Their descendants—people like me—feel a strong pull back to this place.

We are lucky to know a lot about our ancestors. Joseph Belcourt, my great-great-great grandfather, was a French-speaking voyageur born in 1779. He worked on contract for the North West Company, paddling from dawn until dusk in huge canoes, and carrying back-breaking loads of furs over land on long portages. As I understand the story, Joseph was working at a trading post in what is now Manitoba when he met three Iroquois voyageurs—Louis Callihoo, Ignace Callihoo, and Ignace Wanyandi—who had come from the community south of Montreal that we now call Kahnawake. The Callihoos and their descendants were also known by another surname, spelled Karaconti or Kwarakwante. A local historian, Elizabeth Macpherson, wrote a book about them in 1998 called

The Sun Traveller: The Story of the Callihoos in Alberta, and her research turned up a lot of information about Joseph Belcourt and his descendants.

The four voyageurs became friends and travelling companions, paddling west to Lac La Biche in 1804 and then continuing as far as the Athabasca River in the Rockies. They decided to leave their first employer to work for the rival Hudson's Bay Company. Shortly after arriving in the West, the four men started families with local Cree or Sekani women, and with the Métis daughters of earlier French-Canadian fur traders and Aboriginal women. We know Joseph Belcourt was working as a middleman, or canoeist, at Fort Edmonton in 1805 when he was about twenty-six years old, because his name appears in the records of the Hudson's Bay Company. In the 1820s he was working at Lesser Slave Lake, where he probably met Catherine L'Hirondelle, a Métis woman twenty-three years younger than him. They lived and travelled together, and started a family, in what was called a country marriage at the time. They married formally in 1844, shortly after the first Catholic priest, Reverend Jean-Baptiste Thibeault, arrived at Lac Ste. Anne to visit local Métis families and begin a mission. Catherine's parents, Jacques L'Hirondelle and Josephte Pilon, asked the priest to baptize all of their children at the same time. In his research for a short book about the history of the Catholic mission, *Lac Ste-Anne Sakahigan*, the Oblate writer E.O. Drouin found records of 103 baptisms and thirteen weddings at the lake in October 1844. It appears that our branch of the Belcourts began to settle around Lac Ste. Anne for at least part of the year.

The Lac Ste. Anne pilgrimage is also an annual reunion
for the Métis and First Nations of western Canada.

PHOTO OB8563 APPEARS COURTESY OF THE MISSIONARY OBLATES,
GRANDIN COLLECTION, PROVINCIAL ARCHIVES OF ALBERTA

The Métis—the word means "mixed race"—are an indigenous people of the West. The early families at Lac Ste. Anne spoke French, Cree, and a combination of the two languages that became known as Michif. They passed on the Catholic faith to their children. When the men had finished their contracts with the Hudson's Bay Company, they became "freemen," or independent fur traders, trappers, and buffalo hunters. Their families travelled widely across the West on buffalo hunts, moving remarkable distances across the Prairies every season on horseback, and together in long processions of Red River carts. They were not the kind of people to settle down, although the priests tried to encourage them to do that. Each year they came back to Lac Ste. Anne to fish. At the time, and for many years later, the lake was full of whitefish. The Métis ran the fishery, and provided timber and other supplies to the traders at Fort Edmonton.

The people of Lac Ste. Anne welcomed travellers
for church services at pilgrimage time.

Like the Callihoos and Wanyandis, more than two hundred Iroquois had travelled as voyageurs to the West at the end of the 1700s. Some of their descendants, including the Gaucher and Gray families, settled between Lac Ste. Anne and Jasper. These people intermarried with the Belcourts and other Métis and Cree families of Lac Ste. Anne and the Fort Edmonton area, in subsequent generations. Together they created a small, close-knit community where neighbours were usually also relatives.

Today it is difficult to imagine that the tiny, rural community of Lac Ste. Anne could be older than St. Albert, a city near Edmonton's northwest corner that is home to fifty-five thousand people. The famous missionary Albert Lacombe arrived in Lac Ste. Anne in 1852, and seven years later, the priests brought three Quebec nuns, Sisters Emery, Adele Lamy, and Alphonse, to work at the mission. As the years passed, and the buffalo herds began to disappear, Lacombe and other missionaries were determined that the local Native people switch to farming. They were looking for more fertile land than the wooded low areas around our lake. Some Belcourts moved with other Métis people to St. Albert with Lacombe in 1861. By 1874 there were forty-one families left at Lac Ste. Anne.

It was about that time when one of the Belcourts—a thirteen-year-old girl named Victoria Belcourt—travelled on one of the last Métis buffalo hunts to leave Lac Ste. Anne before the hunt ended forever. One of her grandfathers was Joseph Belcourt, the old voyageur. Her great-grandfather on her mother's side was John Rowand, the powerful Hudson's Bay Company chief factor who was the boss at Fort Edmonton until his death in 1853. At seventeen, Victoria married Louis Jerome Callihoo. They had thirteen children, and she lived to be 104 years old. She did not read or write; however, when she was an older woman, and very well respected, she described early Métis life at Lac Ste. Anne in detail in published interviews. I have included two of her stories at the back of this book, because they describe what life was like for our ancestors at Lac Ste. Anne in the late 1800s.

The first pilgrimage to Lac Ste. Anne happened in the summer of 1889. The priests recorded miracles and healings at each pilgrimage, including a note in 1891 that mentioned my great-grandmother. She was born Constance Letendre, and she married Magloire Belcourt. The priest's note said: "Bedridden for six months and who is unable to walk, is carried into the church. She too gets up and walks out on her own."

I suppose if you believe in something hard enough it will happen, because the healing power of the mind is amazing. If you bring people together, believing, it is also amazing how powerful that belief can be. I have heard it said that the lake was always believed to have healing powers, and that the Church took advantage of this ancient belief and adopted it.

To me, the Lac Ste. Anne pilgrimage is a reunion: for friendship, and for storytelling, as you walk around the tents and motorhomes. I enjoy listening to the stories and the laughter. People use the opportunity to earn a few dollars, selling hot dogs, hamburgers, pop, ice cream, old clothes—it is like a garage sale, sometimes. Some people are bargaining, and I find it quite humorous. Does it hold any spiritual meaning for me in a Catholic religious sense? No, it does not. There are times when it reminds me of my thoughts as a kid, when the priests played poker. Selling their beads. Selling their holy water. To me it was like gambling. The pilgrimage is important to me, but in my own way. I think of it as an important gathering for Native people.

I think I am a spiritual person, though. My beliefs are a bit different, more like Lesley's. I feel comfortable with the White Eagle Lodge she attends. It acknowledges Mother/Father God. It is an interfaith group, but more Aboriginal. I believe in reincarnation. I believe in intuition. I believe in God. I believe all religions are sacred. They are like a wheel—a wheel has a hub and it has spokes. Together they form a circle. Each spoke to me forms a different religion, but the centre, the hub, is God. All spokes lead to the hub. All religions lead to God.

When I learned I had prostate cancer, I consulted two medicine men. One medicine man had a vision before I spoke to him that the cancer would not be in my bones. The other medicine man gave me natural herbs and held

The Métis of Lac Ste. Anne.
PHOTO OB8555N APPEARS COURTESY OF THE MISSIONARY OBLATES,
GRANDIN COLLECTION, PROVINCIAL ARCHIVES OF ALBERTA

pipe ceremonies for me. At one ceremony there were about thirty people in a living room. The medicine man spread his blanket on the floor in front of all of us. He said a prayer in Cree. He lit the pipe and passed it around the circle. Everyone took the pipe and asked the Creator to heal. We smudged ourselves with the smoke. When the pipe came to me, and while I was smudging myself, I heard wolves howling. Once I passed the pipe on, the howling stopped. The medicine man said I would be cured. At home, I took part in a ceremony to thank the Creator, honouring the four directions. This I do believe.

I believe in the power of prayer, too. Many people all over the world prayed for me within their different religious beliefs. I am so grateful to them. I am sure the combination of medical treatment, herbs, and prayers contributed to my healing.

I hope Albertans will protect Lac Ste. Anne, because it has a significant place in their history. We should

In the 1930s, hundreds of people arrived at the Lac Ste. Anne pilgrimage in crowded cars, open farm trucks, horse-drawn wagons, and on foot.

rebuild the older buildings, and let the people see what it was like in the old days. Establish a site like Métis Crossing, near Smoky Lake, a proper historic site. Lac Ste. Anne should be protected and rebuilt with statues or sculptures to honour the true Métis pioneers of the early days—the Belcourts, the Letendres, the Cunninghams, and all the others—to make it a special place not only for Native people, or the white people who come to the pilgrimage, but for all people.

I hope young Métis people will keep the traditions of Lac Ste. Anne alive to give them a sense of hope, and a sense of belonging.

THE BELCOURT FAMILY: 1890—1914

The Belcourt family of Lac Ste. Anne posed for at least twenty-two formal portraits in the studios of Edmonton's pioneer photographers after 1890. Here is a small selection from the Ernest Brown Collection at the Provincial Archives of Alberta. Unfortunately, not all family members can be identified.

Magloire and Constance Belcourt, my great-grandparents, with one son, around 1895.
PHOTO BP-2-7622 COURTESY OF THE MUSÉE HERITAGE ST. ALBERT

My great-grandparents, Magloire and Constance
Belcourt, with two adolescent sons, in 1910.

PHOTO BP-2-5832 COURTESY OF THE MUSÉE HERITAGE ST. ALBERT

The Belcourts in 1904. Front row, left to right: Jean-Baptiste "Mooswa"
Letendre, my great-great-grandfather; Constance Letendre Belcourt and
Magloire Belcourt, my great-grandparents. Back row: Jean-Baptiste Belcourt,
my grandfather, as a young man, and unknown family members.

PHOTO BP-2-2775 COURTESY OF THE PROVINCIAL ARCHIVES OF ALBERTA

My grandparents, Marie Rose Laroque Belcourt
and Jean-Baptiste Belcourt, as newlyweds.

My grandparents with three of their children, early in their marriage.
From left to right: Isador, Margaret, and Wilfred, my father.

Unidentified Belcourt family members at the turn of the twentieth century.

Mary Belcourt and her children.

Unidentified Belcourt family members.

My parents, Wilfred Belcourt and Florence Courtoreille
Belcourt, on their wedding day at Lac Ste. Anne. My mother
was fifteen when she married. My father was twenty-two.

CHAPTER TWO

Born a Belcourt

I WAS BORN IN A SMALL shack behind the pool hall in Lac Ste. Anne on July 6, 1931. There were no doctors in the area. A Native woman, a midwife and medicine woman, helped my mother with the birth. Her name was Mrs. Letendre, but everybody knew her by the name of Kiskatas. She picked herbs and medicinal plants in the bush. I remember that she would put drops of coal oil in our throats when we were ill, or we would swallow the coal oil with sugar, just a drop of coal oil in the sugar, and that was supposed to cure a cold. If you had an earache, they would blow tobacco smoke into your ear. I remember this very distinctly, and we laugh about that today, blowing smoke in a child's ear, but that is what they did. It is amazing to me how many children that woman brought into the world at Lac Ste. Anne, and how many she cured of illness by going out into the bush and getting the herbs and roots and making these teas and that sort of thing.

My mum and dad's first little house was very small.

The way my mother described it, it couldn't have been more than twelve feet by twelve feet, made out of slabs of wood. She said in that first fall, when I was a little baby, they had a cookstove, but there was no insulation on the building whatsoever. She went to McConnell's Store and got cardboard, and then she put the sheets of cardboard between the two-by-fours of that little house of ours to keep it a little warmer. She once told me a story about this time. "You always woke up at five o'clock in the morning for a bath," she said, "and I would have the stove red hot at midnight and the water would be boiling. When you woke up, wanting your bath, the water would be frozen solid, and I would have to put the fire back on and reheat the water." You know, it must have been terrible for them in the winter. It is hard to fathom how people lived in those days, but I like to think they were happy, newly married and with a new baby.

My mother's name was Florence Victoria Courtoreille. I know very little about her side of the family, because her own mother died in childbirth when she was born in 1914. She was raised in Alberta Beach by her Aunt Sara and Uncle Gordon Courtoreille. I assume my parents met at the dance hall at Alberta Beach. In the late 1920s and 1930s, there was a dance hall there with a wrap-around porch on it, like a hallway, right near the water. As a child I liked that place. People would gather to watch the couples dancing in the middle. My parents liked to go dancing there when I was young. As I look at their wedding picture, my mother looks to me like a little girl, and that is what she was. She was only fifteen years old when she got married. My dad would have been about twenty-three, as he was born in 1907.

A traditional log house at Lac Ste. Anne, like the Belcourt family homes of my early childhood. Only a few remain in the community today.

I have a childhood memory of my mother as very tall, but actually she was a short woman and quite slim in those early days. She always wore colourful dresses, never slacks or coveralls, but a long dress that would go down below the knees. At times, she wore a kerchief on her head, but whenever she went out, she wore a hat. All women wore hats in those days, and I still think a hat looks beautiful on a woman.

My mother was always working, and that is how I will remember her. Her first baby, a boy, died at birth, or possibly he was born too premature to live. I was the second one, and she had ten children altogether—six girls and four boys, who are all alive today. After I was born in 1931, Ken came in 1933, Gilbert in 1934, Georgina in 1936, Gordon in 1938, Virginia in 1940, Marie in 1942, Josephine in 1944, Viola in 1946, and Patsy in 1947. This was the typical size of a Métis family at Lac Ste. Anne in those days.

My mother had to work very hard to take care of all of us. She patched everything that we wore, patches on top of patches. When we had holes in our socks, she would darn the socks with wool. When the socks fell apart for the last time, she would make them into mitts, cutting the toes off, and sewing them into a new shape. Nothing at all was wasted. To make our clothes, she would cut flour sacks and sugar sacks and sew them together. She would dye the cotton, or bleach it to make our white shirts. Even my dad had white shirts she made for him. She sewed everything for us by hand for years before she got one of those sewing machines with a foot pedal. That must have been a happy day for her.

She was a very clean person, immaculate, and she put a lot of value on cleanliness at home. We always lived in log houses with six-inch planks on the floor, but you could eat from the floors in her houses, they were so clean. We had to take our shoes and boots off at the door. She expected my sisters to work just as hard, inside and outside the house, to keep our family going.

My dad's name was Alfred Wilfred Belcourt, but he was known as Wilfred. He was a strong and dominant sort of person, very intelligent although he had only gone to school until he was in Grade Three. That level of formal education was common in Lac Ste. Anne when he was young. It didn't hold him back in his time.

Dad's whole life was about making a living. When I was very small, he worked as a farm labourer around the area. The farmers would want all of the willows out of their fields in the low-lying areas so they could plant wheat. Cutting the willows, getting the roots out of the earth, and burning the branches and roots, all of this was called grubbing. My father told me he was sometimes paid as little as five cents an hour for this work during the early part of the Depression. He would also go brushing to open up the land, for other farmers, and on our own place. He would cut down the poplars, trim off the branches, and make brush piles to burn. I remember once when I was very young, the brush piles were still smouldering, and I walked on top of a big poplar log. My younger brother Ken climbed up on it and sat down, and he said: "This is nice and warm." Suddenly his pants caught on fire! I grabbed him, and we ran across to a little slough covered with ice—it is a wonder we didn't fall through—but I couldn't put the fire out. I ran to the house for my dad. He grabbed Ken and shoved him into an outdoor tub with ice in it, and of course that put out the fire. My brother was burned badly.

As little boys, we had to learn how to cut wood. Dad had a sawhorse, where you would put the wood down for cutting with a saw, and it was broken. I decided I would repair it. My brother Ken didn't want me to pull it apart to fix it. We were both very small. He put his finger on the cross of the sawhorse. "Take your finger away," I said. "No," he said. He didn't want me to ruin it. Anyway, I swung the axe and I cut his finger off at the first knuckle. Oh, the turmoil! My mother came running from the house, hearing the sound of Ken's crying. I remember him running to meet her, holding his bleeding hand in the air, and yelling: "Herb has cut my finger off!" My mother grabbed him, stopped the bleeding, and began to search for the piece of missing finger. My dad found a neighbour to take us to the doctor in Stony Plain, but it was too late to stitch the finger back together.

It is interesting that we remember the terrifying moments of childhood most clearly. When I was two, apparently, I wandered away from home, the way toddlers sometimes do, and I was gone for four or five hours. Everyone in Lac Ste. Anne was looking for me. I had gone away with my little dog, and the people eventually heard the barking and found me. When I was three or four, I went with my parents to visit my mother's relatives. They had a goose. This goose grabbed me from behind, caught my hair in its beak, and pounded me with its wings. The adults came running to save me.

I do have another vivid memory from my earliest years, an interesting day when I was five. My father took me to visit his friends on the Alexis reserve. There used to be a ferry, operated by a fellow by the name of Hughie Jones, and he would take us to the Narrows. When we arrived, I saw some people were playing cards on the riverbank. A woman was playing cards while nursing a baby in a papoose, pushing her breast back so the baby could reach it. I remember watching her with some fascination, especially when she said, "I raise you," and put money in the middle of the blanket. I heard these little pups squealing in the box of an old wagon, too, and I was shocked when one of the pups tumbled out. It turned out they were wolf pups.

When I was very young, my parents spoke to one another in Cree, French, and English, all mixed together. Their conversation would stop in French, and they would go on in Cree, and continue in English. That was a normal thing in our community. I never did learn to speak Cree by itself, but I recognized Cree words. At Lac Ste. Anne, the Cree was like a mulligan stew, all mixed up with French, the Métis language they call Michif. Today when I hear people speak Cree, I can understand the general meaning, but it depends on where they are from. Once I listened to a Cree tape at the University of Alberta, and I did not understand a word of it. If the speaker comes from northern Alberta or northern Saskatchewan, I can hardly understand at all unless they speak slowly. There is a lot of humour, a lot of laughter, inside the Cree language, and I love that about it.

We moved to different houses around Lac Ste. Anne quite often in my early years. The second house was also only one room. We had a garden to feed us all, and a couple of cows. My parents did not have a car or truck, but few people did. I have a child's perception of these places, and my life at that time. These houses did not look small to me, then, or crowded, although they must have been. Now I look back and say: "How did we live there?" There was an upstairs in that second house, a loft, but the house had no staircase like we have today. We climbed a straight ladder, poles cut out of the bush, and the bark stripped off, and wood nailed for the rungs. Downstairs there was a large table and a wood-burning cookstove, a cupboard, and one bed. There were two beds upstairs. That's all.

I don't remember many toys. My grandfather made a kind of bobsled for us with runners. We had a toboggan. I remember my mother making teddy bears out of old clothes, stuffing them with cloth. We liked games more than toys. We used to play Cowboys and Indians in the wheat field. We made slingshots to hunt for partridges, and we snared rabbits and fish. We always had small dogs to play with us, too. Our friends, the Wickstrom kids, whose parents were Swedish and good friends with my parents, spent all kinds of time with us.

I always wanted a violin as a boy, a fiddle. Somehow I guess my father earned the money, and he gave it to me on Christmas morning. Oh, I was so pleased. It had had a special case. I put the violin on the floor when some people came to visit, and someone stepped on it and broke it. That was the end of my plan to learn how to play some music.

THE MÉTIS PEOPLE are great storytellers. Neighbours used to come around to our house in the evening, and that was our storytelling time. We were told, as kids, to sit on the floor, against the wall, and listen. Our neighbours would tell stories that would make the hair on the back of your head stand up. They talked about the northern lights, for instance, saying you had better not whistle at the northern lights because they are the dead, and the spirits will come down to you. You know, we were kids, so we were tempted. We would go outside in the night and whistle in the darkness, and sure enough the waves of light and different colours in the sky would come and dance closer and closer. Let me tell you—we were scared! They got so close that we could hear the "shh, shh" sound. These are the stories those people would tell, and they would talk about werewolves, too, but there were always some very humorous stories.

My grandfather and a Mr. Campbell used to try to outdo each other on their stories. One funny exchange stays in my mind.

Whenever my grandfather came down the road, Mr. Campbell walked to this wooden gate to meet him and tell him a story. One day he said: "I was down south last fall, and I was working for this farmer, and he grew cabbages so huge, the leaves were so big, that whenever it rained, you got under a leaf to stay dry. That's how big those cabbages were."

So my grandfather couldn't top that. He walked on to Mr. McConnell's store.

The next week my grandfather walked along the road, and Mr. Campbell came back to the gate. My grandfather told him this story about how he went down to eastern Canada, and he went to a foundry, and they were making a cast-iron kettle. Twelve men stood around the lip of this kettle, using sledgehammers to make a roll along the edge. It was so big that when one man slammed his hammer down, the sound would just reach the other side when the second man slammed his hammer. "That's how big the kettle was," my grandfather said.

"So," Mr. Campbell said, "why in the world would they make a kettle that big?"

My grandfather replied: "They heard about those cabbages in Alberta!"

Many Lac Ste. Anne people used to come over to our place on Friday and Saturday evenings, in summer and in winter. My mother would make tea and sandwiches for everyone. We would sit on the floor along that wall, all around the room as I told you, and the adults would sit in the chairs to tell stories, and sometimes they would have a dance. Oh, they could play the fiddle! They would do the jig. My mother could do the jig like nobody else. Some people would jig back and forth across the

Storing sacks of coal for the winter.

room, so quickly, and then somebody else would take over. It was great. I wish I could do it today. Not so long ago, Trevor Gladue, the vice-president of the Métis Nation, and his wife, Felice, came to perform with a Métis dance group at a harvest dinner at Festival Place in Sherwood Park. He got me up, but I couldn't do it anymore. I like to remember those evenings at Lac Ste. Anne.

My only regret is that my dad and mum did not allow us to participate in conversations, as children are encouraged to do today. I think we needed that skill in life, and I did not get that chance at all, not even in school. I think it was sad in a way. I am the type of person who doesn't interrupt. If people are talking away, I will not jump in. I listen, you know, and I fall back into those old ways so many times. I find it hard to get into conversations. I speak briefly, and to the point, and yet I would like it better if a conversation could just flow, like in this book. This is something children need to learn at home.

Everything was quite different for children then. I will never say it was perfect. Our parents expected us to stay at home. We went to school and to church, and then we came directly home to do our chores. They did not allow us to go to the lake to swim, and we rarely went as far as the communities of Lac Ste. Anne or Alberta Beach or Gunn. We never went into Edmonton, or anywhere else. We went to school, and we came straight home because we had a job to do.

They taught us how to work hard—and we worked a lot, my brothers and my sisters—but I do have some fond memories of that time with my dad and mum. In the month of August, it would be haying time. We had to cut the hay, and bring everything to the barn, you know, and make the haystacks out in the field. I remember my mother coming out, in the middle of the hot afternoon, to this great, big poplar tree in the middle of the meadow. She would spread a blanket over the grass in the shade. We would all sit around on this blanket and have our tea and sandwiches, and these were our happy times. I love to remember those days. Dad would go out to the field with the horses, and he would show us how to rake to make windrows. Today, when I go to an agricultural museum with all of the old farm equipment, I understand each piece of machinery and I feel good about that.

All of our food was our own, too. During the summer, when the berries came out, we would stop along the road to pick them. We would pick the wild strawberries or raspberries. When blueberry season came, we had to walk a long way to an area where the blueberries grew.

We would make sure our pails were filled with saska-toons, chokecherries, gooseberries, all that sort of thing. My mother and my grandmother preserved all of these berries, as it was our only fruit for the winter. They worked constantly on that. My mother would also tell us to go into the woods and get a partridge, or to snare rabbits. Sometimes she would make a stew, but some of the meat was cooked and preserved in sealer jars. I hated that stuff for a while. It tasted horrible. I can taste it right now. I could never eat it again.

We also ate dried fish, and sometimes neighbours would bring us moose meat. They would bring us the dried meat in strips, big slabs of it, a foot wide. My mother also made some treats for all of us. I used to love bannock, but there was also another kind of fried bread, about an inch thick, and in a square, that was wonderful. She would put the dough into the fat, and fry it until it was a little crispy. The smell of that bread is just beautiful. If I go to Fort Edmonton Park today, and see them cooking this wonderful fried bread, I love it. For a breakfast treat, my mother would break up dry bread and mix it with warm milk and sugar, but mostly I remember oatmeal porridge every morning. I could not eat porridge for years after I left home; I was so tired of it. I don't understand why we didn't have apples at Lac Ste. Anne. We grew cucumbers, beets, carrots, peas, and lots of potatoes. We had marrows, and turnips to cook with butter and pepper. Everything we grew, we ate.

The women kept everything going. They raised the kids, made the food and clothing, kept the house; it was not the fathers. The men were out there in the world, trying to get a few extra dollars to buy food, to farm,

My Uncle Albert Cadre and Auntie Christina, and cousin, Rosemary, in their garden at Lac Ste. Anne.

and to raise all of these kids. They must have been very tough people in those days.

It was a small community where families knew one another very well, over generations. We had our memorable characters, too. There was a bachelor, Bill Salberg, who lived near us, in a small cabin with a dirt floor. He had one window, one chair, one table, and a little cot. His blankets were horse blankets. To feed his fire, he would just push wood into the ten-inch hole at the top. He never washed his dishes. I remember his cup was so dirty,

Our horses working on the farm at Lac Ste. Anne.

the only white place on the mug would be where his lips touched the rim. He lived with his cattle and sheep, like a hermit, you might say. His little house burned down one day. We heard about it, and I remember jumping on a horse, maybe I was twelve, and I galloped as fast as I could to his cabin. It was too late. His home could not be saved. They were all log houses in those days, and the danger of fires was very real. The Belcourts were fortunate in that way, but some families lost their lives and their homes. My great-uncle, William John, lost his life when his tent burned down while he was on a fishing trip. This was a great tragedy for our family. His son, my Uncle Alex, and his grandson, my cousin John, were both there at the time.

Our meeting place was McConnell's Store. It was one of those old-fashioned general stores, with a porch across the front, made of huge planks, and there were big barrels outside. One barrel had something the consistency of tar in it—molasses, maybe—and I used to go and take a chunk to chew. There was a gas pump outside the store. Inside, a long counter stretched across one wall, with groceries behind on shelves. I would go with my mum and dad. They had credit, a book in which the McConnells would write down their purchases of tea and sugar. They would settle the bill later, when they could. My younger brother, Gordon, has a deep interest in local history and a lot of information. He has kept some of the old bills that people signed for McConnell's Store.

When I was about nine or ten, we moved to a home we called the Sixteen Acres, about five kilometres west of Lac Ste. Anne. This property wasn't very big, of course, and my parents farmed it just for our own use. We lived off the land. We had a large garden for vegetables, and we had six or eight cows. We ended up with a dozen cows for milking, and my brothers and I did that job, and also fed the animals. We had to separate the cream from the milk, and Mother kept the cream to sell because that was her money. She would ship this cream by the can, and we would take it to the highway to be picked up. We had no refrigeration in those days, but we had a well. We would keep the cream can down there because the water would keep it cold.

Our horses were very important to us. I remember a horse called Jim, because he pulled the buggy. He had a curved neck and a tail that looked beautiful when he was prancing down the road, but he was too quick for a child to ride. My favourite horse was a young colt by the name of Bird, who had a star on his forehead. That horse would follow behind me, sometimes nudging me with his head to get me to walk a littler faster, to fetch water from the well, or whatever. Once I was riding Bird, and we were going down the road about a mile, I suppose, around a curve in the road. On the side, a cow trail turned off the road where you could take a shortcut, and Bird decided on a whim to take it at great speed. He went through a kind of tunnel in the trees. I ended up facing backwards on the back of the horse. I fell off, and the wind went right out of me. Bird stood over me, nudging me as if to say, "Come on. Get up." He was a real friend to me.

THE SIXTEEN ACRES was right off the main road between Lac Ste. Anne and Darwell, kitty-corner from my grandparents' larger property of 160 acres. The Belcourt family had built three identical log houses many years earlier. One belonged to my grandparents; one belonged to another relation, Alexis Belcourt, who lived on the next quarter-section; and one was William John's house at Lac Ste. Anne, the only one still standing today. Logs for these homes were all cut by hand, and the corners were fitted. When I was young, these houses were whitewashed.

I can still walk into those log houses of the 1930s in my imagination. As soon as I walked through my grandparents' front door, I saw the wood stove. There was always hot water on the stove, it seems, in summer or winter, and the copper boiler as well. On the right was a big kitchen table, a wooden table almost eight feet long, where everyone would sit. My grandmother always had a brightly coloured tablecloth on the table—yellow, I remember, with flowers. There was a cupboard for dishes, and a window. Beside the kitchen there was another room, a living room, with a stand-up, cast iron wood heater. My grandparents had a gramophone—an old record player with a crank for music—but they also had a radio with

My grandparents, Jean-Baptiste and Marie Rose
Belcourt, as I remember them in their old age.

a big six-volt battery. Oh, that was the best thing in the
world! It was like television for kids today, perhaps more
entertaining for us. I used to like listening to the Lone
Ranger and Tonto. You could just see this Lone Ranger
on his white horse, and this Indian, Tonto, on his Pinto,
and the story played itself out in your head as if it were
a book. We would sit and listen to the stories and then
go to bed.

We would climb a wooden staircase to a second storey
of the house, going up from the kitchen, and find three
small bedrooms up there.

My grandfather, Jean-Baptiste Belcourt, had a big
moustache, and he always curled and waxed the ends. He
worked in the garden, planted the grain, cut the hay in
the fields for the cows. His left leg was permanently bent
a little bit, and he used a cane. He wore denim overalls,
or a kind of heavy felt pants, and I wonder how he could
move in them. On his feet he wore moccasins and toe

My grandfather, Jean-Baptiste, in Edmonton late in his life.

rubber boots that covered the top of the foot. He smoked a pipe he made himself, either a corn cob pipe or a pipe made from a branch. The men would cut a branch, and push the brown core out with a wire to make the hole in the pipe. I liked my grandfather a great deal, and he told me many things I remember.

Once, when I was small, I was making a lot of noise upstairs in their house. My grandfather was trying to talk to my grandmother downstairs, and I must have been stomping my feet above him, because he became annoyed with me. He came upstairs to pick me up and take me outside, and I figured I was going to get a good swat with his cane. He hadn't quite reached the top of the stairs when I grabbed his moustache and held on to it. I slowly turned him around. I think he probably allowed me to do this, because I led him down the staircase by the moustache, and across the kitchen. My grandmother was laughing her head off. I reached the door and ran like hell.

We had no electricity or natural gas in the first houses. We used coal oil lamps for light, and you could barely read by them. When my parents and grandparents eventually brought in kerosene lamps, I remember thinking: "Oh, they are so bright!" We had no running water in those houses, either, so we had an outhouse for a bathroom. When I was a young boy, the family would sit down for dinner together, and then it was time to relax. And where would I go to relax, to be by myself? I would go to the outhouse. It was a two-seater, and on the door was the carved-out shape of a moon. It was a place where a kid could meditate. I would go to the heavens—from this planet to Mars and the moon, and beyond. After several minutes, I would come back to earth. I would look up at the moon and say to myself: "I wonder when Dad and Grandpa are going to put a roof on this old outhouse."

My grandparents' house had a large yard, and farm buildings, also made of logs. They had a house for the wagons and buggies, just like our garages for cars. People still used horses for transportation and farm work at that time. My grandparents had cutters of different sizes, a single buggy and a double-seater, saddles, and work harnesses, all in that building. They had a separate milk house where they separated the milk and cream. The barn was quite far from the house, up high and fenced. Between the barn and the house, a little creek crossed the yard; we had one bridge to go to the barn, and another to the house and farmyard. They had a big garden, too, with basic vegetables: carrots, beets, onions, peas, and potatoes. I don't remember ever selling vegetables. We gave away a lot.

MY GRANDMOTHER, MARIE Rose Belcourt, was a very religious Catholic, a churchgoer. Like my mother, she was meticulous about cleanliness and order in her life. Everything had to be just so; even the harnesses on the horses had to be well polished or oiled. She would go to church at least twice a week—my grandfather would go on Sunday, but she would go in between. I would have to go with her to the church at Lac Ste. Anne every time. I don't know why she chose me. Perhaps I was her favourite, or perhaps it was because I was the oldest, and she wanted company. The church was very small, as you can see today, but in my young eyes it was huge, and full of lots of people. My grandmother expected me to learn the catechism and go with her, no excuses. The worst cold weather didn't matter. In the wintertime, she took a cutter; she had a second one pulled by two horses, and they'd prance as they were going down the road. In the summer, she drove a small buggy in the week and a larger one on Sunday. I became an altar boy. Many years later, I saw the old priest, Father Calvez, and I reminded him: "Do you remember, Father, when I spilled the wine on the white cloth when I was an altar boy?" I remember him standing behind me, hands in the air, praying.

The church at Lac Ste. Anne was the centre of my grandmother's life.

I was supposed to pour the red wine into the chalice, and I guess I was distracted, and I spilled some on the white cloth. Well, he never missed a beat. He knelt down, kissed the white cloth, and slurp—he drank it up! He was a great guy, that priest. He lived into his nineties.

My dad never went to church, except for funerals. He used to encourage all the people in Lac Ste. Anne to go to church, however. One time, someone asked him, "How come you keep pushing this church? You never go." He was well-known and respected, but he would not go to church for anything. "Well," he would say, "I want you to go to church and put your money in the plate." You see, he played poker with the priest. They were very good pals, and my father didn't have to go to church to keep it that way.

Once a year, my grandmother and I would go together to the big church in St. Albert. Father Lacombe's body was kept there, and I remember she told me he was there under the glass—the body—and it was very scary for me as a child. I did not understand why they were preserving him. She told me he was a saint.

I don't know how much of my Catholic upbringing influences my way of thinking today. I suppose it taught me honesty. I have always believed that my word or my handshake is my bond. Beyond that, I have mixed feelings about my Catholic experience in childhood. I remember, when I was an altar boy at Lac Ste. Anne, every Sunday the priests requested money, even though the people at the time only had pennies, nickels, and dimes. This turned me off. I went to confession. I couldn't understand the questions, or the need for them. The priest would ask: "Did you commit this? Did you commit that?" Adultery! I didn't even know the meaning of the word as a boy. This turned me off the Church. I went through the motions, but it was a joke, really. My father and his sisters, Margaret and Christina, and his brother Syd were not religious either. I think my grandmother's piety put them off. She took her religion to great extremes: eating fish on Fridays, fasting, avoiding dances during Lent, giving things to others and going without herself. One of my aunts, Margaret, told us that she would feed roast chicken to hungry visitors while her own children ate potatoes. This was her belief. Her religion had strict rules. The Anglican church I go to now is not so authoritarian as the one I attended as a child. People are more involved in the service. The priest at the Anglican church is a woman. Susan talks about God loving all of nature and that we must take care of our earth. So, I find it comfortable being there. I find God more in nature, now, as our Native ancestors did.

I THINK I started school when I was about seven. I liked school, actually. At first, I would go to the one-room schoolhouse in Lac Ste. Anne, riding a horse, or in winter, my dog, a German shepherd named Rex, would pull me on a toboggan. The weather in the winter seemed so cold then—the temperature could dip lower than minus thirty—and yet we would still take our horses, still take our dogs, to school. I remember I always had a horse blanket to put over the horse's back. Bird would stand there for six or seven hours, waiting for me. In the afternoon, let me tell you, that horse would just gallop as hard as he could because he had been freezing outside in the snow all day.

We carried a lunch bucket to school, a three-pound lard pail. My mother packed baloney sandwiches, something basic, no other meat or fruit. These lard pails served many purposes, including berry picking in the summer. At school I loved to play softball and rugby. In the summer, most of the kids ran barefoot, and the soles of their feet would be like shoe leather. They could run like deer on a gravel road. For some reason, I could not do that. I had to wear shoes on my feet.

The school at Lac Ste. Anne was bright and cheerful. The whole east side of the building was windows, so we had the sunshine. We needed the big wood stove in winter, and we had a cloakroom for our heavy coats. Our desks faced a wall of blackboards, and we were lined up in rows according to our grade. The smaller children would listen to the teacher's lessons for the older ones, so we were learning and reviewing all the time as the years went by. It was a good system, I think, and a lovely school. When I went back a few years after I left home for good, it was gone.

There were too many children at the Lac Ste. Anne school—Native children and white children—and the school was just too small. So the Belcourt kids went to another one-room school, made of logs, in the country to the west of the community. This was the Beaudry School. The war was on by then, and it was hard to find teachers after our first year there. They closed the school for a time. For the next two years, I didn't go to school at all. I went back when we finally found a teacher, a Mrs. McCormack, who remembers that I liked history. Even so, I felt I was so much older than the other kids, and so much bigger than my classmates in the same grade. I guess I felt ashamed, so I began to think about leaving.

I didn't learn anything about Métis history in school: nothing about the fur trade in Canada, or Louis Riel or Gabriel Dumont, or anything at all about western Canada. It was all European history at that time. That is what they were teaching. Today it seems so sad to me. I had no idea about my family's history at all, not until much later.

Sometimes other kids called us half-breeds at school, and that made me feel dirty. It didn't happen that much, because the Belcourt kids mixed quite well, but I do remember it. Kids are kids. My sisters remember the schoolyard racism of that time, too, and the fights they had over it. As I grew up and became a teenager, I heard all of those things, too. By the time I went out to work, I was ashamed of my heritage. Why? I just don't know. I guess because I felt dirty in the eyes of others. We were all known then as "half-breeds," and maybe it was the word I didn't like. You would want to say to people: "I've got French blood in me, like, part French," to try

My brother, Ken, front right, and me, top left,
with our friends Mervin and Vinty Wickstrom.

A class at Beaudry School in the 1940s.

and get away without answering the question that you're a Métis, as we are called today. What will we be called in another fifty years? Will we be just characters in an old storybook by then? I hope the racism will disappear in the decades ahead.

It wasn't until 1958 that I said to myself: "This is stupid. This is me. Accept me for who I am. If you don't, it is your loss, and not mine." I took that attitude as a young man, and I never looked back. Words can sting a child, however, and no matter how you come to terms with racism as an adult, you don't forget the hurt of it.

I left school at the age of fifteen to go to work.

CHAPTER THREE

Voices Across the Water

THIS IS A MEMORY OF an earlier time in my childhood, long before I left home. It was the fall, I remember. My mother asked me to take a lunch pail out to my father in the field. My dad was working in a farmer's wheat field with a grub hoe, day after day. I was a younger kid then, and the wheat was over my head, blowing in the wind. I used to pretend that the grain field was the ocean, and that I was moving through the waves. When I arrived with my dad's lunch, he sat down on this brush pile, and took a long sip of his tea. He was wearing a white undershirt. I remember the sweat rolling down his face. The memory stays with me because I think it taught me something important.

"When I finish this job," he said to me, "I will never work for another man as long as I live."

He swore, in fact, and he never did this as a rule in front of his children.

That day, when my father finished the brushing, the

farmer paid him a five dollar bill for several days' work. He came home and said to my mother: "I'm going to the store to change my five dollars into nickels and dimes. Then I'm going over to the reserve to buy muskrats, because Albert Cadre is coming through here soon, and I'll sell him whatever I buy." He went to the Alexis reserve, on the other side of the lake, and within five minutes, he was broke. He had no idea how much to pay the trappers, so he paid five cents for small muskrats and ten cents for big ones. When Albert Cadre came by Lac Ste. Anne and bought these furs, my dad doubled his money. That was phenomenal for our family. When Cadre left on his fur-buying route, he said he was coming back a few days later, because he was taking out my dad's sister at the time. My dad couldn't wait to go back to the Alexis reserve to buy more muskrats, and then sell them to Albert.

After these sales happened a few times, my dad thought to himself: "Albert must be making money on me." The next time he went to the reserve, he bought the muskrats and took the Glenevis train into Edmonton. He found out he could sell the muskrats at fifty cents each if he sold them directly in the city, and he had only been selling them at twenty cents to Albert.

"I don't think you can buy my muskrats anymore," Dad told his friend the next time he walked in the door. He told him the truth about what he had done. Albert flew off the handle. He grabbed the money out of his pockets, and threw it on the floor. "Money is your God!" he said, because he was so mad. After that, Albert started buying furs around the country for my dad. Their roles had reversed. Soon my father had built up quite a solid reputation in Edmonton among the independent fur buyers.

The trouble was that he was buying fur to support his growing family, but he did not have a license. This was called bootleg fur, and it was not allowed. The game wardens were always after him, trying to pinch my father, but they could never find the muskrats. I remember one time—I think Ken and Georgina were with me—when the game wardens came into the house to surprise him. Mother, of course, put some wood in the stove to make tea for them. They were sitting around our table, and it was covered with a tablecloth. The old tables at that time had a special cupboard, built underneath the surface, where a family could keep the cutlery. The game wardens didn't realize that my dad had hidden his furs in that cupboard, not too far away from their knees. They sipped their tea and left.

This is when we were living in a one-room house with two beds. Anyway, someone must have heard about where my dad was hiding the fur, because the wardens came back again at night. Mervyn Hearn, the game warden in that area, was frustrated because he still couldn't find it. My dad was well-liked in that community, and all the people were helping him.

Whenever people saw the game wardens on the Lac Ste. Anne Trail, they would go to the lake and holler, one person to the next person, in Cree: "The game wardens are coming, the game wardens are coming!" I remember in the fall of the year, through the fog, those voices calling to my father in Cree. It is a beautiful sound to remember.

The game wardens kept coming. My dad suspected

someone had squealed on him, or something like that, because he went to the priest and said: "Will you help me?" So the priest agreed to help hide the furs, and guess where they put them? Behind the altar in the church! I was an altar boy by this time, at my grandmother's insistence, and I remember seeing these big bags sitting underneath the altar table, with the white cloth to cover everything up. They never did catch my dad with his furs.

He had another early warning system, too. My dad was a good friend with a Mr. Forsland, who was the head man at the government's game branch in Edmonton. This Mr. Forsland would phone McConnell's Store at Lac Ste. Anne and leave a message: "Tell Wilfred Belcourt that I called." It was a signal to everyone that the district game wardens were heading our way again. Everybody would holler in Cree, running around, and the priests and the Catholic brothers would grab the furs from behind the altar, and hide them in the hayloft in the barn.

My father worked as a fur buyer steadily after that. At first, he would walk long distances to reach the trappers, all the way from Lac Ste. Anne to Lake Isle and beyond, and he would walk home carrying heavy loads of fur on his back. He told me he would bring a small hatchet and sleep out in the bush, cutting spruce boughs to use as a mattress and to make a fire. He would walk from one community to the next to find the trappers, and he would be so weary when he came home. He did well, though. I remember the day he brought home his first Model-T Ford, our first car at a time when almost nobody at Lac Ste. Anne had a car. He was so proud, and Mum was proud. The wheels were high, with quite a clearance, which he needed on those mud roads. Even then, he had to find someone with a horse to pull him out of the mud more than once.

My father stayed in the fur business—eventually, with a licence—until his death in 1976. He worked for years in a successful partnership with an independent Jewish fur merchant in Edmonton named Sheppe Slutker, and we got to know Mr. Slutker's family very well. My dad trained some of the Belcourt children in the business, Ken, Gilbert, Gordon, and Georgina, in particular. Later, my brother Ken started Ken Belcourt Furs, a successful business that endures today, selling fur that goes to China and all over the world. I have asked my family members to contribute a chapter to this book in order to pass on their substantial knowledge about the industry.

A tradition that goes back centuries in the Belcourt family—the buying and selling of furs—continues in an unbroken way. The fur business has been important to Native people all across Canada, and to many other Canadians, too. Families have relied on it, and communities have grown strong because of it.

I am proud of this tradition, but I did not choose the fur business for myself. I never did believe in the killing of animals, and I will tell you why. When I was a boy, a farm neighbour was butchering an animal, a cow, and he asked me to take the gun and shoot it. I did what he told me. This cow stood and looked at me after I had pulled the trigger, and the tears were rolling down from its eyes. I swore I would never kill another animal again, and I don't think I have ever done it to this day. I just refused.

A few years ago, my wife, Lesley, wrote a story about the way the Métis people who lived around Lac Ste. Anne helped our family in the 1930s with warnings about the game wardens. I have included her story at the end of this book because she tells it so well.

I like to think of the sound of the Cree voices across the water, not just as a warning, but also as a reminder of our strength when we help one another.

CHAPTER FOUR

Moonshine

MY FATHER DECIDED TO GET a still to make moonshine. I suppose he was listening to the priest when he said: "Go into another business or profession."

I used to go with Dad into the bush away from the house to look at the twisted pipes. For days, he kept going back there to check on his still.

One day, as he was tasting the moonshine, he said: "Mmm, it's good. It's ready."

He went home and found a one-gallon wine bottle and he filled it with the liquor. He took this jug to the creek, where he was brushing land for a farmer. He found a bend in the creek, with the grass growing over the bank and the water flowing underneath, where he could hide his gallon jug.

"Only God could find this!" he said.

A few days later, he went back to check on his moonshine, but it was gone.

Heading for home, he became suspicious that Billy

Letendre, who was also making moonshine, had taken it. So he followed Billy for a few days.

Billy made a full gallon of his own homebrew and took it quite far from his still, to a clump of willow trees. He set the gallon in the middle of the willows. That night there was a terrible storm. My dad took an empty gallon bottle and replaced Billy's full gallon with the empty one. Then my dad took a stone, threw it at the empty bottle, and shattered it. He went home.

The next day, another storm began with lightning and thunder. The lightning split a big tree in front of our home. Billy Letendre came along. As my dad sat with him at our kitchen table, Billy asked: "Have you ever heard of lightning striking and smashing a bottle?"

My dad chuckled. "What is a bottle? Just look at this big tree that the lightning shattered."

Billy left our house still thinking the lightning had struck his bottle of moonshine. My dad did not tell him what really happened until ten years later. They had a good laugh about it, and Dad said: "Now we're even!"

CHAPTER FIVE

Leaving Home

I LEFT HOME IN LAC STE. Anne for the white man's world at the age of fifteen, and never went back.

I suppose we were such a big family—with so many aunts and uncles, brothers and sisters—that it was only natural for me to go to work as soon as I was able. No one encouraged me to stay in school. I had reached the age of manhood, and I was looking forward to beginning my own life.

A kid knows when it is almost time to leave home. One day, Ken and I were in the barn and I saw my father approaching us. I must have done something wrong, because he waved to me to come to him, and I could see his finger pointing at me. "Okay, Dad," I said, but under my breath I muttered something. "Today is the day I am going to take a round out of you." I was fourteen. Anyway, the closer I got to him, the bigger he looked. Soon he looked like a giant. I turned around and started running towards the old railroad grade, hoping to jump through a square space in the fence near the tracks and follow a path through the bush. I ran for all I was worth, with him about five steps behind me. He picked up a willow switch as he was running, and I could just see the leaves flying from this willow. Somehow, the mind works quickly, and I decided that I couldn't dive through the hole in the fence, but would put one leg through first, and then my head.

I got stuck in the wire fence. My backside was sticking out on one side, and my head on the other, and I could see Dad. He couldn't help it. He had to give me one hell of a licking with that stick. Then he helped me get out of this fence, and he put both of his hands on my shoulders. "Now, son," he said. "If you ever think that you can take a round out of me, you stand up to me like a man." And my dad and I got along perfectly after that.

This was in the years following the Second World War. Many young men from Lac Ste. Anne had gone to war, and some had lied about their age in order to enlist. My cousin Joseph and I tried to join the Canadian military, and we lied about our age. They gave me some papers for our parents to sign, so I went home with these papers in my pocket. My mother went through my clothes and found them, and she became very upset because she thought I had actually joined up. Dad looked at these papers. He didn't say a word. He crumpled them up in his hand, walked over to the wood stove, and threw them in the fire.

"That's the end of your army career," he said. "Did Joe sign up with you?"

"Yes," I admitted.

"Let's go," he replied without another word.

At fifteen I left Lac Ste. Anne to work in logging and mining camps.

We jumped into the Model-T Ford, and he drove over to his brother's place and walked in the door. "Where's Joe?" he said. "Syd, did you sign those papers?"

"Yes," his brother said.

"Where are they?" My uncle handed my cousin's enlistment papers to my father. Once again, he crumpled them in his hand and threw them into the stove.

My father had other ideas for me. It was time for me to leave home and make my way in the world. One day, he drove me to catch the bus south of Darwell, about ten kilometres from Lac Ste. Anne, and he lectured me all the way.

That was the longest ride I ever had in my life. I have never forgotten his words. "Save your money and work for yourself," he said, "or you will be carrying a lunch pail for another man for the rest of your life."

The Cree word for the Métis people is *otipemisi-wak*—roughly meaning, "the people who work for themselves"—so maybe my father's strong belief in self-employment sprang from his Métis culture, as well as his own life experiences. My uncles and aunts were always telling me this, too, before I went to work: to save my money. Of course, being a young boy, I didn't have the guts to tell my parents, uncles, and aunts that they were full of baloney—not to their faces. I didn't dare tell Dad that he didn't know what he was talking about.

Looking back over the years, I understand that my dad was right. He didn't mean it as a father's lecture. It was something he knew and he was telling me the truth to the best of his ability. I will always be grateful to my dad for that. He drove me south of Darwell to Carvel Corner on Highway 16. The bus stopped at the local store there, a little bit west of Wabamun, and I climbed on for the ride to Marlboro, Alberta. I had a job lined up at one of the Swanson Lumber Company camps. I caught a ride on a logging truck that was heading into the bush, about thirty kilometres off the highway, into this logging camp.

I arrived at my destination around midnight. The bull cook, the man in charge of the kitchen and the bunkhouses, showed me where I would sleep. I walked into this building to see a big oil drum converted to a heater. It was red hot. Five men were snoring in their bunks, and the room stunk to high heaven. You could just about throw up—it was that bad. "I'll go and get your mattress," said the bull cook. He went away and I sat on the edge of this wooden bunk, looking around. He came back with a fork of hay. He scraped the oil drum, the heater, as he went by, and the hay sent out sparks. He threw this mess onto my bed. He spread it out and said, "I'll go and get your blankets and pillow." He brought two Hudson's Bay blankets, and a pillow made out of canvas and filled with feathers. "Have a good night's sleep," he said, and off he went.

Well, I hardly slept that night. This bunkhouse was so lousy, with bed bugs and lice, you didn't have to fluff your bed. The lice and bedbugs could fluff it for you, as if to say: "Oh, there's going to be a meal here!" I sat on that bunk, thinking about the home I had just left for the first time, and asking myself why I had ever left. It was such a clean home, with white sheets, such a wonderful place. I think I fell asleep crying.

The first morning we had breakfast—a beautiful breakfast, fortunately. They took me over to the sawmill

Aunt Margaret and her son Ron Robinson in Mayerthorpe.

and they put me behind the saw. They were sawing approximately eighteen thousand feet of lumber per day. My job was to pick up the lumber as it came off the saw, and make separate piles of different lengths: eighteen footers, sixteen footers, ten, twelve, eight footers. It was a constant run, taking this lumber away from the saw. You must remember it was green lumber, quite heavy, but I was a strong lad and able to handle the job. When I received my first paycheque in two weeks, I discovered I owed them money! They took two dollars a day for room and board. I was a young man, going into the company store for the first time in my life to see pop, chocolate bars, pants, clothes, gloves—everything I had never been able to buy for myself as a child. All I had to do was sign my name. Well, that was easy. Come payday, my purchases came off my cheque, and I owed them a fortune. "Don't quit, Herb," said the foreman. "I'll give you a different job."

They gave me another job, carrying railroad ties at another sawmill, not too far from the same camp. The ties were heavy as they came off that saw. I had a pad on my shoulder, with teeth on it, to help me shoulder the load. As the square timber came off that saw, you grabbed it. The wood hit your shoulder and you ran with it. You had to make a stairway, as you piled these ties up. We were working ten hours a day, six days a week, with only Sunday off. Two or three workers would get sandwiches from the camp on Sunday, and go trout fishing at a little creek there. We would have a fish fry in the bush, and then come back for dinner. I was able to handle the job, but one day I said to myself: "This is no life for me. I will never save any money here." The other workers were men in their thirties and forties, country people, a great bunch of fellows, and they looked out for me because I was the youngest. Even so, my father's words were in my mind, and I could see I would never achieve anything doing this type of work for long. I decided to move on.

Heading west again, I went to the Coal Branch in the foothills of the Rockies, what they call Mile 48, south of

Hinton. I ended up in a coal-mining community called Cadomin. When I first arrived, I went to the local mine office and they hired me. I went up to the bunkhouse, and my God, it was like a palace. The floors were clean, washed. You had your own room. You had a clothes closet. Your bed was made for you. It was absolutely clean. I sat on the edge of that bed for about twenty minutes and said to myself: "I can't take this job, because I'm lousy. I'm full of lice and bedbugs." So I walked back to the company office and I said to the superintendent, "I apologize, but I can't accept this job." He wanted to know why. Wasn't the accommodation good enough? "Oh no, it's great," I said, and then I told him with embarrassment that I had lice in my hair, and probably bedbugs in my clothes from the last job. He laughed, and said: "Don't worry about that. I'll put you in a job where the lice and bedbugs won't live for a day. I'll put you up at the tipple."

A tipple is where the coal comes up the mine, like a chute. Three men on each side sort the rock from the coal. The coal dust was so thick the light bulbs looked orange, and in those days there were no health regulations that I could see. I will tell you, at lunch hour, the only things white were my eyes and teeth. I could chew the dust in my mouth, and I'd go out and cough the dust out of my chest, then have a shower, eat sandwiches, and go back to work again after lunch. We worked eight hours a day, and then had another shower and change of clothes before going back to our rooms. Cadomin was a friendly community in a beautiful landscape. To my surprise, I found I had an uncle and aunt there, Ed and Girly Cunningham, from the large Métis family that settled between Lac Ste. Anne and St. Albert. I boarded with them, but I stayed in the company bunkhouse at night. I lived like that in Cadomin for one full winter. I tobogganed, did some skiing—just about killed myself in the mountains, skiing behind a car down the highway in two metres of snow, but it was lots of fun.

Working conditions at the strip mine were much better than at the sawmill. The cleanliness was great, except for the tipple. I only stayed in the tipple for about a week, and the superintendent was right. After the first day, I didn't have any lice. Nothing could live in that! It is a wonder I am still alive! Anyway, they put me outside working the night shift. I kept the tracks in line, extending the lines, because they were loading the coal cars. I think I have some pictures of me standing on one large steam shovel somewhere, the great big shovel that picks up the coal. In a disaster one night, a mining accident buried one of the men under the coal and water. It took us several days to find him, and by this time, his body was bloated. The smell was so bad, it stayed with me for years.

I was a coal miner for a year. One day I saw a job advertisement on the local bulletin board for MacGregor Telephone and Power, an Edmonton company looking for linemen. A lineman is a worker who climbs telephone or power poles, and strings wire to connect a telephone line or power line to a house. I thought I could do the work, so I rode into Edmonton for an interview. They hired me right away, but I had to go back to the mines to give them notice. I have always believed in giving notice to my employer. On July 6, 1947—my sixteenth birthday—I went straight to Riley, Alberta, to start a new job that would teach me a new skill and push me toward true independence.

My six sisters and my mother. Left to right, back row: Viola, Georgina, Virginia, Patsy. Front row: Marie, our mother Florence, and Josephine.

CHAPTER SIX

Sisters

SISTERS OUTNUMBER BROTHERS IN OUR family. I left home not long after my youngest sisters were born, and in a way, I am still getting to know them. I asked them to tell me about what their lives were like after I set out on my own.

My brothers and sisters have followed different paths in life. As we get older, these many paths lead back to a place where we can be together. Their life experiences, and their memories of our family in Lac Ste. Anne, are an important part of the story I am trying to tell. I invited them to my home one day in April to ask them for their own perspectives on our family, and the stories of our shared heritage that we need to preserve together.

Georgina, like me, remembers our early homes in Lac Ste. Anne in the 1930s. "Grandma Belcourt was a nice lady," she remembers. "She tried to teach me to speak French. When I was a little girl, I spent a lot of time at her place. She could speak Cree fluently, and French fluently. She had been born in Montana." Georgina also talked about the steady berry-picking in the summer, a chore that all the kids remember. "I remember Mum, picking berries, canning, finding raspberries late in the fall. She sent us out picking. Once we found a raspberry patch on the bachelor's land, Bill Salberg's place, and we picked them all, filled our pails and ran home. 'Where did you find those?' Mum said. 'Out in the bush, Mum,' we told her. If she had known, she would probably have made us take back every one."

As the oldest daughter, Georgina defended the younger Belcourts from bullying at school. "I wasn't happy in school," she said. "I was glad when it was over. I got out at sixteen. I remember a lot of discrimination. The teachers were okay, but some of the other kids were beating us up. I think the name-calling came from their parents. Where else would children learn it? Kids aren't like that today. Red, yellow, black, they don't make a difference. I think some of the children who went to school thought we were intruders. There was a lot of name-calling and bullying." Georgina worked in many jobs after she left home: in a dry-cleaning plant at first, and then cooking in restaurants in Edmonton, Valleyview, and Nipawin, Saskatchewan. She married Peter Kosick, and in 1965, the family started a construction company in Edmonton. Peter's company, PK Construction, built the bridge over 50th Street at 107th Avenue in Edmonton. Georgina became a bookkeeper for this family business, and she managed the accounts for my father's fur business, all while raising five children. "Every Belcourt knows how to work," she said. "There's not a slouch in this family. All our family, our children, are hard workers."

Marie explained our family's decision to leave Lac Ste. Anne in 1956 after so many generations in one community. She said her father and the older boys were always away buying furs, or working around Alberta. "Mum was tired of living in the country. There was too much work for just us girls. Virginia milked cows, pitched hay, cleaned the barns. Georgina was inside, helping Mum with the indoor jobs. When she moved, Mum loved living in the city. She said she would never patch another bed sheet. She would go to bingo at the Rainbow Ballroom and the Knights of Columbus hall." Marie stayed in Edmonton and raised three children, and she is the only one of our family who has a great-grand-child—a four-year-old girl she is raising.

All of my sisters share strong memories of my mother's influence on us. Virginia was born on the Sixteen Acres, and moved with the rest of the family from Lac Ste. Anne into Edmonton when she was sixteen. She became a clerical worker in several downtown businesses, and after raising three daughters, she now lives north of the city in a community called Cardiff. "All I remember is Dad buying furs and cattle, and being away on fur-buying trips, and Mum raising us. She was beautiful. She had a hard life, I know that." Marie added: "In those olden days, men were the boss, and you did what you were told. Now things have changed. I am the boss of my own life."

Josephine talked about my mother's experiences with childbirth. "Mum never talked about her life. In those days, they didn't. But I know that before Marie was born in 1942, a midwife came from Lac Ste. Anne to help my mother with the babies. After that, my mother had the rest of her babies in the hospital in Edmonton.

Dr. Weinlos delivered us." Josephine married Andy Dolan, who worked with me at Mutual Phone Line Servicing when he first left high school. He stayed with me when I started Belcourt Construction in 1965; he later became a partner with the company. Josephine and Andy built the second house in the large suburban community of Mill Woods in south Edmonton, and raised two daughters.

My younger sisters have different memories of the languages spoken in our home. "Mum wouldn't speak Cree in front of us, because she didn't know a word of English when she went to school, and she said that was so hard," Marie remembers. "That's why she wanted us to know English right from the start. She never taught us Cree. She and Dad would speak Cree together when they didn't want us to understand something, but not to us."

As one of the youngest Belcourts, Viola remembers glimpses of farm life. "I do remember that my grandmother said the rosary every night, and listened to church services on the radio in French. She chased us away when she was eating. I remember playing in the hayloft, making little rooms in the hay for houses, and rolling down the hills when I was very little.

"I remember my life at home later as work, work, work. We had to bake bread every day and scrub the floor with lye and a brush. We washed clothes on scrub boards, and heated up the iron on the wood stove. We learned to cook full meals on that stove. Our mother did not teach us these things. We taught ourselves by watching. We had much more to do after the age of ten.

"When we moved to the city, we faced a little discrimination, but not much. I think in those days—in the 1950s—people were subconsciously ashamed of being

Native. Today we go back to the Lac Ste. Anne area, and everybody acts as if we were always their best friends. It wasn't always like that when we were in school." Virginia added: "Some of them thought they were going to beat up every Belcourt. They thought they were King Tut. Sometimes I remember a teacher would call us 'dirty Indians,' and the kids would want to fight, but Georgina would look after us."

Pat is the youngest sister. She was only nine years old when the family left Lac Ste. Anne for the new home in the city. Still, she likes to remember playing with Viola in the hayloft on the farm. "Georgina helped Mum with the younger kids," she said. "I don't remember my older brothers at all at home—not Herb, Ken, or Gilbert—because they left home so early. I did live at home with Gordon, because he was younger. When the older boys were gone, Virginia worked outside with my dad on the farm work. She was really strong, and she liked that work better than inside work. I remember when the snow was very, very deep, Virginia would carry me on her shoulders to Darwell School."

Some of the old Belcourt family traditions continued after the family moved to Edmonton. My sisters remembered that our parents were strict, especially with teenage girls, but they also talked about our mother's strength and commitment to her family, and our father's generosity in his successful years in the fur business, late in life. "My dad used to tuck hundred-dollar bills into my cigarette package to help me out," said Pat. "Once he bought me a fur coat." Every Sunday the brothers and sisters, and their spouses and kids, would gather at our parents' home in Edmonton for a dinner of roast beef and lemon pies. They played cards and told stories. "Dad would give our kids a dollar to come and give him a kiss. They would line up in a row to kiss him."

Our parents felt fortunate to have come through the harder times of their lives in Lac Ste. Anne. "They would tell me stories about that time," said Pat. "Once when they were first together, and Dad wasn't in the fur business yet, Mum wanted to go dancing with him. It cost seventy-five cents to go. My dad worked for a farmer, pulling tree stumps, for a week to get that money to take her. They went dancing and came home with ten cents."

Our parents were married for forty-five years. Their children, and most of their grandchildren, live in the Edmonton area.

"I think we are all pretty close, especially now that we are older," says Pat. "If we had our disagreements, we could always forgive, and come back together again."

CHAPTER SEVEN

Working for Myself

ALBERTA WAS A GREAT PLACE to explore in the late 1940s and 1950s, if you were a young person looking for a job. The province was much more prosperous than it had been when my parents were starting out during the Depression, and I guess it has been a lucky place ever since. I turned sixteen just a few months after they discovered oil at Leduc, and my generation has had more opportunities than any previous one in Alberta.

The electrical business was booming in 1947. Every Alberta farm family wanted electricity—many of them still had no power—and there were no machines in those days to drill holes for the power poles. They hired young guys like us to dig the holes by hand. The average pole is more than ten metres tall, and we would have to dig a two-metre hole to sink it into the ground. We worked with something called a spoon and bar. Try to imagine a big spoon with a long handle on it, and a long bar, both taller than a big man. We would scissor this spoon and

In Edmonton, early 1950s.

bar together in a movement, pulling back and forth, to dig the hole. It was good exercise for building muscles, believe me. In eight hours, I could dig the holes for fifteen poles, depending on the earth. If it was hard clay, we moved slower.

I believe I was earning sixty cents an hour for this work in 1947, but that was good money then. We ate in restaurants, and we could buy a T-bone steak and all the vegetables for eighty cents, with the steak so big it would cover the platter. We slept in tents from April to September, and then we moved into local hotels for the winter. I was not old enough yet to go to a bar in the evenings, so I would go to play pool, or go to a movie for twenty-five cents. The linemen moved all over the province, following the work. I remember how cold it was in the winter, riding in the back of one of those two-ton trucks. The back of the truck was covered, but unheated. We would run the muffler inside this "caboose" to keep us warm. Thinking about it now, I realize how dangerous it must have been.

I was travelling around Alberta for the first time in my life. I stayed in the eastern part of the province for about a year, and then I moved steadily south for almost four years. When I left the company, we were building a transmission line from Canmore, in the Rockies, to the BC border and the US border. The line went right across the mountains in a southwesterly direction between Montana and the border of the state of Washington.

We were living in tents in the mountains in the fall when it began to snow. We were soaking wet, right up to our hips, working all day and coming home to a wet tent. I was so cold. We would take off our pants and hang them up on lines inside the tent. We had a little heater in there to try to dry off our clothing, but it wouldn't dry well. We would eat our supper in camp, fall into bed dead tired, and of course, the stove would go out. In the morning, we would get up in the frosty cold to pull on the same clothes again. Sometimes our pants were frozen when we got into them. It was wicked.

"If you can't change this type of living, I'm leaving," I said to the foreman, and I left. I went to Mr. Strachan, the superintendent for the company, to tell him about my decision.

"What are you doing here?" he said. I told him I planned to quit, and he didn't like it.

"You'll be back," he said. "All of you linemen quit and come back."

I looked him straight in the eye. "No, I will never be back," I said. "Not unless I come back as a competitor one day!"

I went to work for Calgary Power—Farm Electric Services within Calgary Power—where I found work as a supervisor for the construction crews. We were building power lines all over the province, and I had a company truck. I felt like a big shot now. I stayed with them for one year. Then I got a job with the City of Edmonton, also working on power lines. I was climbing poles in the city, but it was very dangerous work. There were no safety rules in those days. We climbed up the poles to these cross arms with all the wires, twenty-three hundred volts at the time, and we had to crawl up between the wires and work these wires at the top. A few men were killed on the job within the year I was there. It was the type of job that didn't allow you to daydream about what

A power lineman in camp.

you did the night before. You had to keep your mind on what you were doing when you were up on the pole. I suppose I was lucky. I was always conscious about safety. I left them and I went to work in Vancouver.

I was married by this time. In 1952, when I was twenty-one, I married my first wife, Olive Laskiwski, a nurses' aide at the Royal Alexandra Hospital in Edmonton. She was born and raised in a Ukrainian-Canadian family at Lilly Lake, just north of the city. Young people used to like to go dancing in the city—places like the Trocadero Ballroom and the Moose Temple were popular places to go—and I believe we met that way.

My work demanded a lot of travel. Olive came with me to Lloydminster, and we rented a house on a farm. We came back to Edmonton and purchased a small house in Jasper Place, an independent town just beyond the western edge of Edmonton, which is now a part of the city. We lived around 153rd Street and 95th Avenue, but from then on I went alone to my work assignments across the West and she stayed in the city. Olive and I had two sons together. David was born in 1953, a very calm little boy, quite interested in the world as he was growing up. He liked to read books about gardening and history. Kim was born in 1955, and he was a happy-go-lucky little fellow. Olive looked after them very well; she was devoted to them. She was also a hard worker, and continued to work at the General Hospital and the Royal Alex after the boys were born.

Our marriage had its difficulties. I was on the road with my work, coming and going, for twenty years. When I came home, Olive wasn't too interested in going out, but she did go, reluctantly. She did her best. Our marriage ended in 1970, and I remember it this way. She always had dinner on the table when I came home from work. One evening I came home and she said: "Well, I think this is it." It was over. I was quite shocked at the time, although I suppose I knew it was coming, but you never accept these things before they happen. She left the home for a few weeks, but came to the house during the day to cook meals for the boys until I found a new place. We spoke to the two boys, told them what had happened. I said I would always be there for them, not to worry about that. I believe Kim was sixteen at the time, and David was eighteen. Their mother never remarried. She has always been a good mother to our sons, and I am grateful for that. I will come back to their story later.

Jobs can put a lot of strain on family life. In the early 1950s, I got a job as a foreman with a large electrical company, so we moved to Vancouver for four months.

They needed a supervisor in Powell River, BC, so we moved there for a year and then returned to Edmonton, where I found work with another electrical contractor, Burns and Dutton.

Working for that company, I made my way up north to Eldorado, Saskatchewan. It was a boom town in the northwestern corner of Saskatchewan, where the border meets Alberta and the Northwest Territories. They were building a uranium mine up there, and needed skilled electrical workers. In the first week, I found myself working for a foreman who was a crude, mean drunk. I couldn't stand the man. One day in the first week, I tore into him for his drinking while we were working out in the bush. I didn't realize that the superintendent was sitting on the hill, listening to my tirade. That afternoon, the superintendent found me and asked me to come to the office the following morning. I thought I had been fired. I went to the office, expecting the worst.

"How would you like to take over the outside work as a foreman?"

His offer surprised me. "Well," I said slowly, trying to think. "I would take the job on one condition. I want the man in charge now out of camp completely. I don't want him around here."

"That's up to you," the boss replied.

I fired the drunk, and stayed for eighteen months. I became the superintendent for the electrical part of the project, even the inside work. It was dangerous work there, too. We had to carry big electrical cables on the emergency walkway down the mine shaft, and they were very heavy. We relied on winch lines to hold this cable as we inched our way down. If it ever let loose, we knew it would take everything down with it: the staircase, and the people to their deaths. We had to be very careful.

I lived in a large and clean bunkhouse, with good cooks in the cookhouse. We could eat all we wanted. Everyone took sandwiches to work, but there were plenty left over in the morning. The cooks would throw these extra wrapped sandwiches on the garbage dump. The local Native people would go to the dump and pick up the sandwiches. This bothered me a lot. I went to see people in charge. "Why don't we just give them to the people instead of throwing them on the dump?" I asked. I was told hygiene rules did not allow the camp cooks to give away food. Once the food was in the dump, it wasn't the company's responsibility anymore. It still bothers me to think about that. What a sad way for outsiders to treat local people.

I made a lot of money in those days. I would collect a paycheque for five or six hundred dollars clear, with room and board. We would be out there for three months before going home. There was a poker game going every night. The day before the men went home, they would get all their money from the bank. They played poker that night. Some men would lose three months' wages at the table, and they would have to borrow money to go home to their families—with empty pockets.

I planned to go on a holiday when I finished the job in Eldorado. I told the superintendent I was going to Winnipeg to visit friends, and I gave him the phone number in case he needed me. When I reached Winnipeg, there was a message waiting for me to call the office. "You've got to get back here," they said. "We've got an emergency in Yellowknife. The power cable to the fuel depot blew up in the middle of the lake."

I flew to the Northwest Territories immediately. Northerners in Yellowknife stored all the fuel for Esso on an island. They needed that cable fixed in a big hurry. In those days, I was considered one of the top cable splicers because of my experiences in Edmonton, and at Eldorado. When I arrived in Yellowknife with the crew, I found a Megger, a tool for measuring insulation resistance and moisture, to help me find the break in the cable. I measured the distance from the shoreline to the place where the cable was broken. We found the location of the break. Pulled by a tugboat, we went out on the lake on a barge to raise the broken cable out of the water. It was heavier than I can possibly describe. We did our best to pull the cable out of the water, but we lost it and it slipped back down.

Frustrated, we had to start all over again. We raised the cable the second time. I went back to the shoreline to get another barge, and went to the island to try and raise the other end of the cable. When we put the two barges together, we found we were short of about thirty metres of cable, so I spliced in a new cable in two places. The splice consisted of a long, narrow box. I had to pour the lead, and build the ends of the box onto the cable. We heated hot tar and poured it into the box to seal the splice and make it watertight. We repeated the procedure at the other end. Finally we connected the cable to the energy source, which carried twenty-three hundred volts.

"We might as well put this overboard," I said to the men. With crowbars, we threw it overboard. As far as I know, the splice is still holding today.

This was a difficult assignment, and I was proud of it. I had only planned to stay a week, but Western Gas hired me as a supervisor to rebuild the local electrical system. My own employer, Burns and Dutton, agreed with this proposal, so I completed the job. After that, my company sent me north again to Inuvik, up near the Arctic Coast in the Northwest Territories. The nearby community of Aklavik was reported to be sliding into the sea, so they had to build a new town. This is what I was told at the time, anyway. I imagine a political angle had something to do with it, another side of the story, because after all these years, the town of Aklavik is still Aklavik. It is still there. They built the new town, however. My job was to build the power lines to the housing sites, all built above ground, of course, because conventional foundations and trenches can't be built in the Arctic region. The planners intended to build an energy corridor, a kind of tunnel above ground, and use steam from the power house to heat the houses. I thought it was quite a good idea, but I couldn't begin to work immediately. I had to wait for the crew and equipment to arrive.

Neither the Canadian government nor the Canadian construction or mining companies on contract made much effort to hire local Dene or Inuit workers for northern projects in the 1950s. The companies delivered everything from the south: supervisors, workers, and supplies. While I waited for the crew, I had a small plane and pilot at my disposal. The plane had pontoons, so we could land on lakes and go fishing. This lovely holiday ended when the crew arrived. Working with the Alberta men, I built the power house and the power lines to the housing site. In the early 1950s, as I remember it, Inuvik had no public buildings except for the church, which was shaped like an igloo. The Protestant and the Catholic

Churches were building two hostels to house children from the Mackenzie River valley over the summer. We had two bunkhouses and a cookhouse for the men. That was it.

My crew worked hard—very efficiently, too—and we finished the job in Inuvik in the early fall. After I had ensured that the equipment was working, the men were paid, and we all went fishing for two weeks. It was starting to get cool, and when the snow flurries started falling, I said to the men: "Let's go. Let's leave for Edmonton." We loaded our tools into the plane and we flew home. When I walked into the Burns and Dutton office the next morning, the superintendent—a redheaded fellow named Sanders—looked up at me with astonishment.

"What are you doing here?" he said. I told him the job was completed. I took out my briefcase to show him the contract papers, all signed by Montreal Engineering. I was quite proud of the fact that we had completed the work in only three months. I handed the papers to him as he sat at his desk.

He was furious with me. He hit the ceiling. The federal government had agreed to pay the total cost on a job estimated to take six months—wages, meals, airfare for the crew, materials—and the company could add on their profit on top of that. We had finished our assignment early, and our hard work made a big dent in the company's expected earnings. When the superintendent lost his temper with me, I became very angry and resentful. In those days, I didn't take anything from anyone. I told him he could shove his job where the sun didn't shine. I walked out of that office without looking over my shoulder.

It was 1958, a critical time in my life. I resolved to act on the advice my father had given me on the day I left Lac Ste. Anne as a kid. I would work for myself. The time had come. I have not worked for another man since.

I OWE MY success in business to a broken kitchen chair. Older people will remember that kitchen chairs in the late 1950s and early 1960s had shiny metal frames and colourful plastic upholstery. In cold weather, the plastic on the seats of the chairs would split, and they looked terrible. This happened at our house. I said to my first wife: "You know, there has to be a dollar in fixing these chairs. I'm going to put an ad in the paper and see what happens." She wasn't too happy about this, because it meant I wasn't going out to work. I put the ad in the paper, and in no time I was swamped with requests.

At that time, the old Eaton's store in Edmonton was selling a new material called Leatherette. It was quite heavy and strong, so I decided to use that. I charged customers six to eight dollars a chair, depending on the style. Soon the basement of that little house in Jasper Place was full to overflowing with Edmonton's broken chairs.

I did the upholstery work myself. Sometimes a brother-in-law or somebody else would come over to help me. When they visited, I would be busy working downstairs to recover these chairs, so they often offered to help. I made more money in three months, fixing those chairs, than I had in a year at my previous job. It was just an idea that worked, and I liked it. I met many fine people in Edmonton. When the broken chairs began to spill out of the basement and garage, I built a double garage as my upholstery shop. That became too small as my business expanded, so I opened a larger shop, Herb's Upholstery, on Stony Plain Road at 151st Street. I started to get work from Alberta government departments, because they wanted their chesterfields in Leatherette.

The oil boom was in full swing in Alberta. Workers on the rigs lived in trailers, and the companies would trade the old trailers for new ones, or fix up the old ones for a new batch of workers. Every trailer has a settee—a cheap sofa or chesterfield—and I remember it took about one metre of fabric to recover each one. The companies wanted the cheapest material on the market, as long as it looked good at first sight. I bought material for three dollars a metre. If you looked at it hard, it would come apart, but they were happy. I made nothing but money on these settees, and there was nothing to it. A seamstress could sew it together in a few minutes, and the upholsterer could put it all together in no time flat. I ran this business from 1958 to 1960, and then sold it, with the idea of doing something new with the profits.

I happened to see an ad in the paper from my old area, the rural district just west of Lac Ste. Anne called Darwell. The district wanted to build a sixty-five-kilometre telephone line from one property to the next, and install telephones in forty houses. I tried to figure out how I could do the job. I owned a half-ton truck, but I had no machinery. The truth was that I didn't own anything that I needed. I went to talk to a local farmer, Pete Hardman. He was the president of Darwell Mutual Telephone Company. I turned around and formed a company, Mutual Phone Line Servicing Ltd., and I put this bid in. They had open bids at Pete's farmhouse, and just two bids came in. Wouldn't you know it? MacGregor Telephone and Power, my old employer, the one I had left saying I would never go back except as a competitor, was bidding against me. You would swear we had copied each other's bid. They were identical. I couldn't believe it. I realized the farmers would give the bid to the larger company with so much experience. They asked me to leave the kitchen. Within five minutes, they called me back.

"Herb, if you can drop your price by fifty cents a pole, you've got the job," they said.

I did not wait a second before changing the price. That was a loss of eight dollars a mile. It wasn't much money. I got the job, I suspect, because they knew my family. They knew me as a hardworking man, and I think people in that area were proud that I was doing well. I didn't want to disappoint them, but I realized I had a challenge on my hands. I had one truck, and I did not even own a shovel. This is when relatives came to the rescue. I had a cousin who owned a company called Sunrise Construction.

"Ron, I need an earth-boring machine," I said. "How much will you charge me to dig holes, sixteen holes per mile, plus the anchorage or whatever is needed?"

"I'll charge you a dollar a hole," he said. That was cheap, I thought. The operator was included, and he looked after his own room and board. I turned around and hired men to do the work. Everyone was local. There were no material costs, except for the black telephones themselves, which I bought from Northern Electric for ten dollars apiece.

First, I hired the men to take the telephone poles out to where the stakes had been placed. They were short poles, and the guys could throw them off the truck by hand. Then I had tamping bars made—a tamping bar is a long piece of pipe, about three metres long, with a flat metal plate like a shoe at the bottom of it, for digging—and some shovels. We installed all the poles along the sixty-five kilometres in a short time. Now we had to connect the line. I didn't have anyone in my crew trained to climb the poles, but as I had worked for the City of Edmonton, I knew linemen. First I hired local farmers to string out the wire on the ground. We took a stick and we put the wire over the insulators and tensioned the wires. To finish the job, you have to tie the wires to the insulators. I went to three City of Edmonton linemen with my offer. "I will pay you, drive you out to the country, and bring you back, if you just tie those wires on during two free weekends," I said. They agreed.

We organized the work like a relay race. I had welded a bar onto the back of the truck bumper, so each man could grab it and jump into the truck as it came by. I kept driving all day, not even slowing down much. I would drop off a man at a telephone pole, then drive back in a hurry to pick up the first guy I had dropped off. We would go on to the next telephone pole, and another man would jump off the truck and scramble up the telephone pole to attach the wires. It was amazing, really. We worked at that high speed for a month. When the telephone line was finished, I hired another fellow to help me install phones in the forty farmhouses. I made nothing but money on that job. After that, I was swamped with telephone work all over Alberta.

The timing for this business was perfect. Everybody in rural Alberta wanted a new telephone. Some still had the old crank system. They wanted modern dial phones, and with so many young people working in the oil patch, rural families could afford these improvements. My new company put in the telephones north of St. Paul, south of St. Paul, all over Bonnyville, Cold Lake, and the Peace River Country. It was amazing how many telephone lines I built before I sold that company. I had a new plan, and it was quite a bit more ambitious.

I wanted to return to power line construction, because that was my chosen trade. With Alberta's oil business booming, and with cities and towns growing, I knew I could build power lines into the oilfields and between communities. I started Belcourt Construction in 1965 with profits from the sale of my telephone installation business. I paid cash for three trucks: a three-ton truck with an earth-boring machine, a two-ton truck for stringing wire, and a half-ton truck. It felt good to pay cash for these trucks, a real accomplishment. Canadian Utilities gave me my first job at Valleyview, Alberta, but I needed a line of credit to start the work.

I had never had a line of credit before. I paid people with the cash I had in hand. I went to my bank, and despite my considerable success in small business and my track record of keeping promises, the manager would not give me a line of credit for twenty-five thousand dollars for several reasons. I refused to give them my house for security, for one thing. I had a family, and I was not prepared to put a home for my wife and kids at risk. On one terrible day, I went to every bank on Jasper Avenue and along Stony Plain Road, from 101st Street in the centre of the city, all the way out to my own neighbourhood in Jasper Place. Everybody turned me down. I was fiercely disappointed. I wondered if their refusal had anything to do with racial attitudes, or unfair assumptions about the way I looked or talked. I kept walking. I was going back home, with my tail between my legs, feeling bitter, when I realized I had missed one bank.

I didn't realize that business people could make appointments with bankers after 3 PM. I went to the nearest pay phone and I called the Royal Bank at 105th Street and Jasper Avenue. I made an appointment to see the manager the next morning at 10 AM.

I was very negative and dejected when I walked into the bank the next day. The manager, Mr. Reyfuse, I believe, told me to sit down. He sat behind his desk and looked at me. We had never met before, and I can't imagine what he was thinking as he stared at this angry young man.

"No, I'm not going to sit down," I said. "You will probably turn me down just like the rest of them."

He looked at me, stunned. I was far too negative, but I couldn't seem to help it.

"Sit down," he repeated. He rang his buzzer, and his secretary came with two cups of coffee. "Tell me about yourself."

I began to answer his questions. I told him where I was raised, about growing up at the farm near Lac Ste. Anne, about all the places where I had worked, and the businesses I had started. I expected nothing from him.

"How much are you looking for?"

I managed to say, "Twenty-five thousand dollars." It was a lot of money in 1965.

"You know, I can give you that," he said. "I don't think you're a bad risk."

I never looked back after that. Over the years, as my company grew and prospered, I ran up that line of credit

I started Belcourt Construction in 1965. When I sold the business
in 1980, the company had 250 employees.

from twenty-five thousand to five-hundred thousand
dollars. I didn't often use the credit, but it was there if
I needed it. Years later, Belcourt Construction got a big
job in Saskatchewan. Mr. Reyfuse was a senior executive
with the Royal Bank in Saskatchewan, by this time. I
told him we had a big job worth a few million dollars,
and I said I needed a one hundred thousand dollar line
of credit from the main branch. "Come in when you're
in Regina and sign the note," he said. It was as simple
as that. I could have dealt with the business from here,
with my office making the cheques out, but I registered
the company in Saskatchewan. We put up power lines
all over that province.

This is what can happen when one banker takes a
chance on one young Canadian.

I will always be grateful to that man.

Belcourt Construction did very well. Through the
1970s, we had a $3.5 million payroll. When I sold the com-
pany in 1980, I had 228 men in the field, plus the workers

in the office and shop—250 people altogether. It was one of the top three companies building power lines in Alberta.

I bumped into one interesting problem at the beginning. That old voyageur in the 1700s, Joseph Belcourt, had left behind some relatives in Quebec. Wouldn't you know it that their descendants would enter the construction business? Belcourt Construction Ltd. in Montreal built office buildings, and the company was huge in Quebec. They wanted me to change the name of my company, and I wanted them to change the name of their company. Only the lawyers in the middle made money on our dispute.

"This is foolish," I said to the general manager one day. "I'm going to put a stop to this." I picked up the phone and called the other company's headquarters in Montreal for some straightforward talk. We reached a great Canadian compromise: Our Belcourt Construction wouldn't work east of Manitoba, and their Belcourt Construction wouldn't work west of Ontario. That ended the legal battle and stopped the sky-high bills.

Business is so risky. I had everything on the line: our livelihood, the well-being of my wife and children. I knew I had to be careful and yet take risks, too. I did not always have the experience or the information I needed to take the next step. I believe in asking questions. There is nothing wrong with requesting advice when you need it, and thoughtful people are usually willing to help. Sometimes, on a business trip, I would say to the stranger sitting next to me on the plane: "This friend of mine asked me this question, and I wonder what you might have to say about it." I would outline the problem, saying I had promised my friend an answer when I returned from the trip. We would discuss the problem, and I would think carefully about the wisdom of the proposed solutions. This proved to be a big help.

I relied on my own business hunches, too. Calgary Power needed a power line between Lake Wabamun and Lethbridge. We bid on the first ninety kilometres. We had to begin the work in January, and I wanted to try something new. To pour the concrete for the footing of a new power line tower, we had to drill four holes. The usual method was to dig with a backhoe, a slow process. I wanted a new kind of earth-boring machine that could dig a much larger hole, much faster. The only place that manufactured that type of machine was in Houston, Texas, and the company wanted $275,000 for the machine. Even if I could afford it, it would also require a large truck with huge tires to carry it. I didn't want to pay that kind of money. I heard that a company had been using the same new equipment to build a portion of a pipeline in Alaska, and that some might be up for auction soon. I flew to Alaska and discovered four of the machines I needed. Two were in huge crates because they had never been used. I bought one for $40,000—a far cry from $275,000—but I still needed to get this monster machine from Fairbanks, Alaska, to Edmonton. A local trucking firm wanted $10,000 US, but I did not want to pay that much. I picked up the phone and at midnight Edmonton time, I called a man named Tony, who ran an Edmonton trucking company. I described the weight, the width, the length, the works.

"We will need a pilot car," said Tony.

"I realize that," I said. "How much?"

He told me it would cost five thousand dollars.

"When can it leave?"

"In an hour," he said. "He'll drive all night." The Alberta crew arrived in Alaska in record time, and we loaded this machine and shipped it back to Edmonton. I flew home and bought a big Kenworth truck, and we put huge tires on the front end of it. We took the machine out to Wabamun, and it cut through frozen ground as if it were butter! That contract was so successful that more business came our way.

Like anyone who is eventually successful in business, I had mentors at the beginning. These people seemed to respect me, and I found them courteous, friendly, and helpful. A few years after I started Belcourt Construction, in 1967, the chairman of the board for Calgary Power invited me to lunch. He told me he had heard good things about my company, but said he thought my company needed an engineer.

I agreed with him, but spoke bluntly: "What engineer is going to come to a small company like mine?"

He replied that Peter Sebzda was one of the top engineers at Calgary Power, and that I should make him an offer. He advised me to invite all engineers working on power projects to two Christmas parties in Edmonton and Calgary. He would spread the word that I was looking for an engineer. Peter came to see me. He did not know I had heard about his excellent reputation. We negotiated a salary, and I offered him 10 percent of the profits before taxes. He was an extremely good man, a fine estimator. I think he was one of the best. He looked for details. As for Calgary Power, I think they realized I wanted to do a good job, at a reasonable cost, and our business relationship would prosper with an engineer of his capability in our company.

Thousands of Canadians work in the northern bush country, finishing tough jobs under extremely difficult conditions, with skills that would astonish people in the rest of the world. You will rarely hear northern power line workers boast about their achievements or their contributions. They just don't do that. Most Canadians live in cities and rarely have a chance to witness or appreciate such abilities. I think these workers deserve our gratitude for tackling the worst of winter and wilderness to bring electricity to rural and remote communities. When my company was constructing power lines in the north, one of my biggest worries was that a generator would quit when the temperature plunged to minus thirty or minus forty. This happened once in northwestern Alberta at a camp we set up between Keg River and Rainbow Lake. One of the men called me to say the generators had quit and the camp was completely frozen. No water. No lights. I phoned an Edmonton trucking company to send a new generator north immediately on an emergency run. Once the generator was installed, we had quite a job thawing out the frozen pipes, and replacing them. That day, the temperature dropped to minus seventy. It is hard to believe! We kept all of the trucks running twenty-four hours a day. When we pulled out of camp in the morning, the front wheels of the trucks would skid, but not turn. That's what work can be like in the north.

I learned quickly how to hire the right people for the job. First of all, I'd shake hands, look the applicants in the eye, and try to get a sense of why these people wanted the job and how hard they would work at it. I checked their references with previous employers and tried to find out if they moved often from job to job, as that was a warning signal. If they came from the province of Saskatchewan, I hired them without an interview. I know we are not supposed to make generalizations about large groups of human beings—positive or negative—but I make no apologies for my hiring policy. I discovered over time that crew members from Saskatchewan were often raised on farms; they were extremely good people, worked hard, and knew equipment. I was rarely disappointed with their work.

I had crews stationed all through that remote area of northern Alberta—around Rainbow Lake and Zama City. I remember another difficult job when we built power lines from Wabamun to Peace River and Fort McMurray. The weather was so bad as the crews started out from Wabamun. They struggled through a lot of swamp. Crossing Lac Ste. Anne at the narrow part of the Alexis reserve, we had to use helicopters to set some of the aluminum towers. It was quite spectacular, watching the helicopters pick up towers and fly them through the air.

About 1973, I got into financial trouble with one job in northern Alberta. We were building a power line from Valleyview to Grand Cache, and it turned out to be one of the toughest jobs my company had ever tackled. When I bid on the job, the right-of-way had not yet been cleared. The territory was all rock, cliffs, gullies, and coulees, and so it was difficult to build a road for our trucks. I went over the territory in a helicopter with the people from Canadian Utilities, looking down at the route for the right-of-way. We could not see several deep ravines, where the trees grew taller. From the air, the landscape gave the impression of gentle, sloped hills. I sent in the work crews to begin the job. They set up a camp for forty men, with generators for electricity. A contractor began to clear the right-of-way with D8 cats, and our crews started building the power lines behind the machinery. We hadn't built more than eight kilometres of line when I realized I was running seriously over our cost estimates. I believe we were more than one hundred thousand dollars in the hole.

I didn't know what to do. Driving up to Edmonton from Calgary, I suggested to my manager, Peter Sebzda, that we might have to close the company down. He was shocked. He convinced me not to give up, to keep trying, and to ask for a bigger line of credit. I told him we would give it a try. At Red Deer, I made an urgent call to our office to speak to our accountant, Gordon Lange. I asked him for the exact cost of the job, even if he had to work all night. The next morning, his estimate was on my desk. Anna Halliburton, the company secretary, had typed it carefully. I was grateful to Peter, Gordon, and Anna for putting this report together so quickly. I knew I could count on them in an emergency. They were wonderful employees and became my good friends. I made an appointment with the Royal Bank and brought up the line of credit to five hundred thousand dollars, and then I took all my costs to Canadian Utilities and renegotiated the contract. After negotiations, they took up the contract and paid me straight cost-plus for the entire job. They gave me a cheque that same afternoon for my shortfall. I appreciated their confidence in me, because they had given me my start in the power line business. I did not want to let them down. Business rclationships built on trust can last a long time and produce significant results.

The next day, I said to Peter, "I'm going out to Valleyview to make some changes." I had to take some drastic steps. I fired the supervisor and three foremen for poor performance, and I selected a competent man from the crew of thirty-five men to be the new supervisor. The job seemed to leap forward after that. The company thrived through the rest of the decade.

As I grew older, I began to enjoy the challenge of starting new independent businesses in unfamiliar areas of commerce. My business ideas usually came from a personal observation or experience—something like the look of a broken kitchen chair.

I HAVE LIVED most of my adult life with my wife, Lesley, and my children and grandchildren, in Sherwood Park, a large and friendly suburban community beyond Edmonton's eastern boundary. When I was fifty-two, I began to see a need for a movie theatre in the community. I phoned the film distributors in Calgary to see if I could get movies. I regret that I didn't make myself clear. I wanted first-run movies. They said there would be no problem distributing movies to a new theatre in Sherwood Park, but they were thinking of older movies, after the theatres in Edmonton had finished with them. I went ahead and built the theatre, the Sword and Shield, with two screens. I put in the latest equipment—projectors, seats, popcorn and pop machines. I phoned the distributors again and said I was ready for the first-run movies.

"No," they said bluntly. "It can't be done."

Apparently, Cineplex and Odeon held a large umbrella over Edmonton, Sherwood Park, St. Albert, Leduc, and Spruce Grove. I was shocked to learn that no independent operator could obtain first-run movies. This was in the era before videos. For a year, the Sword and Shield ran older movies for children and young families. Our program was very popular, but I remained determined to bring in fresh movies. I travelled to Toronto to meet with the head distributors in Canada, people who represented Columbia, Warner Brothers, Universal, MGM, and Buena Vista. I heard my first "no" from the Warner Brothers representative at 9 AM, so I immediately invited him and the rest of the distributors to a meeting the next day at the Royal York Hotel. Meanwhile, I phoned our premier at the time, Peter Lougheed, and asked if he could help get rid of this invisible umbrella over Alberta. His people phoned the film distributors. I also phoned Peter Elzinga, my MP in Ottawa at the time, and he too agreed to help.

The next morning at 10 AM, the distributors arrived at the meeting. They had put away their umbrella! It would be wide, blue skies over Alberta after all. Most were willing to distribute first-run movies to our theatre, with the exception of Buena Vista—the company that distributed the Disney movies. Apparently, Famous Players had a monopoly on the films. This bothered me. I came back home, and a few weeks later I decided to phone Buena Vista in Los Angeles. I spoke to the vice-president, and he asked me if I would be attending a movie convention in Las Vegas in a few weeks. We agreed to meet for lunch there to discuss the Sword and Shield Theatre in Sherwood Park, Alberta! We had a great conversation, and after two hours, he said: "Herb, here is a phone number. From now on, you deal directly with our distribution office in Los Angeles." We paid 20 percent less for the films by going direct. We never looked back after that, and we had a great relationship with all of the distributors. They would phone and ask us to take their movies.

I remained worried that Cineplex and Famous Players would move into Sherwood Park as competitors. I became the president of the Movie Theatre Association in Alberta. Famous Players and Cineplex said they would not come into Sherwood Park until the population reached one hundred thousand people, a big relief for me. They kept their word.

Our theatre grew to four screens, with 930 seats. A few years later, the Onyx Corporation from Toronto put in a theatre in Sherwood Park Mall. They had one theatre in Toronto. They put in twelve screens here, so we eventually ended up closing down our local Alberta-run theatre. It was another signal to me of the beginning of a change in Sherwood Park. It had stopped being a small community where citizens preferred to patronize locally owned businesses. Today, we have very few local businesses in a much larger community. They are mostly large American-owned chains or franchises. However, local businesses now occupy the old Sword and Shield building, and use it for office and storage companies. I enjoyed my work in that theatre.

I WONDER WHAT my religious French-speaking grandmother would have thought if she had known that I would one day open an English pub—and have a bit of fun with our family name on the sign! The Bell and Court Pub and Restaurant was a great adventure in business for me.

I had visited the pubs in England and I liked the friendly atmosphere in them. They were places for people to meet their friends, enjoy some entertainment, share a good meal, and walk among the tables to greet others for conversation. That's my kind of place, and nothing quite like it existed in my community. I did a survey of the number of British people who lived in Strathcona County, around Sherwood Park, and it turned out to be 30 percent. I applied for a "roving licence," the first one in Alberta, which would allow customers to stand while drinking. The new Bell and Court Pub and Restaurant became a very popular place in Sherwood Park. We had eleven British beers on tap, a first in Alberta. We had piano singalongs and entertainers such as The Chancers, an Irish group; a comedian/pianist, London Booby; soloists and many others. The place was always packed, but nobody got drunk. People came from all over the Edmonton area and outlying communities. The Bell and Court replicated a true British pub in décor and atmosphere, and visitors from Britain would often tell me that it was so much like their local pubs.

One evening, two elderly ladies came to the door and stood still at the entrance.

"We just wanted to have a peek," they said. "We've never been in a bar."

I tried to invite them to stay. "This isn't a bar," I said. "This is a home away from home. We just happen to have two seats by the fireplace. Come on in and sit down."

"But we don't drink," they said.

"You can have tea or coffee, or non-alcoholic drinks," I replied.

They plucked up their nerve, entered, and ordered a pot of tea, which was served with its own hand-knitted tea cozy. They read magazines by the fire with pleasure, and nothing terrible happened. Later they became regular customers, and other seniors followed.

In the restaurant, we organized afternoon strawberry teas with fashion shows tied in with local merchants. Once a week, on Tuesdays, we offered a Dinner and a Movie special tied in with our Cheap Tuesday movie prices at the Sword and Shield. At lunchtime, people came for the bangers 'n' mash and other specials. My good friend Don Enyedy and his wife, Yvette, never missed a lunch for years.

When we finally sold the Bell and Court, I received a call from the Alberta Liquor Control Board commending the operation of a well-run pub. "We did not get one complaint about drunkenness or rowdiness," they said. "If all bars were run like this, we would not need the inspectors we have today. Congratulations!" Five years after we sold the business, the Bell and Court Pub moved to another location, but Oscar's Pub was created in its place. A British-born couple, Fred and Trish Underwood, have welcomed customers to Oscar's for twelve years, and it remains very popular.

I started several other businesses, some successful, some not. I opened Lord Belcourt Formal Wear on Jasper Avenue in 1970, with my son Kim as manager. We built up an extremely good business, renting tuxedos and accessories for a decade, before I sold the business. I had the measurements of some of the cabinet ministers in the

Lougheed government. Whenever they needed a tuxedo, their secretaries would phone and I'd have it delivered. The business is still running under the same name.

I sold Belcourt Construction to some of my employees in 1980. The new owners were Peter Sebzda; Gordon Lange; my son David Belcourt; Mel Speraka, a truck driver; and Lee Gursky, Bob Bogle, and Andy Dolan, who were supervisors. My brother-in-law Andy had been working with me from day one with the telephone installation company. There was an economic downturn in Alberta in the early 1980s. Fifteen years later, the new owners wanted to retire, and they decided to close down Belcourt Construction, laying off ninety people in a single day. That was a sad day for me, very emotional, because I had started that company from scratch.

That's what I like to do. Start something from scratch.

CHAPTER EIGHT

Creating Homes in the City:
The Story of Canative Housing

OFFERING AN AFFORDABLE HOME TO a family is deeply rewarding work. I look back at the rich and complex story of Canative Housing Corporation with pride and gratitude. I have earned a good living in a long career in private business, and these businesses provided the comforts I have today. Yet Canative Housing, a non-profit corporation, gave me the added pleasure and satisfaction of successfully helping Native people in many different ways, a privilege and honour that I could never measure in money.

Three men—not one—sustained Canative Housing through three decades of hard work and problem-solving. Georges Brosseau, Orval Belcourt, and I worked as a team. We were more than business partners; we were loyal advisors to one another, a trio of shareholders committed to the same goals. I don't think Canative would have succeeded without the combination of our different talents and perspectives.

Georges Brosseau, Orval Belcourt, and I worked as a team at Canative Housing.

Georges Brosseau is a lawyer who grew up in a strong Métis family in northeastern Alberta. His father, Alphonse Brosseau, was a business owner in St. Paul and an early organizer with the Métis Association of Alberta in the 1930s. His Métis mother was a member of the L'Hirondelle family. Georges earned arts and law degrees from the University of Alberta, and started his own practice in Edmonton. He has excellent business sense and a deep commitment to the well-being of the Métis people.

Orval Belcourt is my first cousin, the son of my father's brother Emile, and like me, his Métis family roots are in Lac Ste. Anne. Orval's brother, Tony, has worked tirelessly for Métis people as a political leader at the national level; he is the president of the Métis Nation of Ontario, and he led a long and successful battle for legal recognition of our hunting and fishing rights. My cousins were raised in a small house on our grandfather

Jean-Baptiste's homestead land. Orval has a strong background and interest in social work. He was the innovator in the creation of the helping services and daycare we offered to Canative tenants.

Georges and Orval are conscientious and gifted men, and I admire them very much. Together we built an unusual non-profit corporation on a pure business model. Between 1971 and 2005, we purchased 179 homes in Edmonton and 49 in Calgary, and rented them to Métis people at realistic but affordable rates. We looked for three-bedroom homes with large basements so that we could renovate them to accommodate larger families. We hired a highly capable manager, Gordon Hornby, who worked with office administrators Sharon Martin, Judy Hilbert, and Vicki Gillis. Diane McLellan joined us in the later years. We had a Métis contractor, Joe Letendre, who made sure that workers had renovated the houses completely before anyone moved in—with new paint, new carpets, yards fixed, and fences repaired. Andy Boyko, an electrician, stayed with us for over twenty years. A Métis contractor, Don Ferguson, did all of our plumbing work. We hired carpenters Albert Hutton and Jacques Denis to build the extra rooms these families needed. All of us were committed to creating something very special in Edmonton, something unique in Canada.

Some people rented from us for over thirty years. Thousands of Métis people lived in those homes at one time or another. We started a food co-operative so tenants could buy food at wholesale prices. People would give us their orders, and we would bring the food to one office where they could pick it up. We did so many things in the early years of Canative Housing. We started noon-hour volleyball games, and organized baseball teams. We created an urban life skills course, intended for the women who did not work outside the home, long before these courses were widely available in Edmonton. When the women said they couldn't bring kids to class on a city bus in the cold winter months, we purchased a school bus to pick them up. We opened a daycare centre on 95th Street at 115th Avenue, a big two-storey house with four qualified workers. We paid for the daycare workers' classes. The Métis bus driver would drop off the children at our daycare, and then take the mothers to the eight-week course. They would often return home in the afternoon with a meal they had prepared in a cooking class. Canative supplied all the food for the class. We organized a Teen Time to provide recreation for adolescents. We helped women sell their Native handicrafts. We brought in public speakers to tell people about educational opportunities in the city, child-raising techniques, where to go for addictions counselling, and ideas for home maintenance.

We tried to offer far more than an empty house to the tenants. We wanted to create a community across the city. We wanted to welcome newcomers in a helpful, practical way. If you treat people right, with respect, they will respect you. Our tenants paid their rent. Sometimes, when they were strapped, we gave them extra time to pay, but they understood our expectations. I tried to make them feel that they were part of this corporation, and that they could not let the Métis people down. That was my motto, and they came through in spades. Our staff was great. In the last five years, our receivables were zero. When we dissolved the company, many tenants chose to buy their homes. We were like a family.

I am proud of these achievements, very proud, and I know that Georges and Orval share my deep sense of satisfaction. Someday I hope a business writer will complete a detailed book about Canative Housing, because I don't think that anything quite like this company has existed elsewhere in Canada. I can only touch the surface of the story in this book about my life, and my family.

PERHAPS A TIME will come in Alberta, and in Canada, when readers will understand why the Métis people needed a housing corporation of their own in the late twentieth century. I hope I live to see that day.

I would like to live in a Canada that has overcome the profound racial discrimination that afflicted the Métis people of the West in the 1960s and 1970s. I want future generations of Canadians—of all backgrounds—to be free of the rural and urban poverty of those years, too.

It is difficult to grasp, even for a Canadian of my generation, the seriousness of the housing problem in the late 1960s. Paul Hellyer, a federal cabinet minister, organized a national task force in 1968 to investigate the quality of urban housing for poor families across Canada. His report in 1969 cited an estimate from the Central Mortgage and Housing Corporation, a government agency, which said five hundred thousand homes in Canada were "defective." Citizens with low incomes occupied most of these houses. The report was shelved, and nothing much was accomplished.

Closer to home, the Métis Association of Alberta conducted a housing study of 1,134 households, containing 6,340 people, in research financed by the CMHC in the late 1960s. The final report provided a shocking look at the housing emergency in Alberta. Forty-five percent of these Métis families lived in three rooms or less; more than a third had a living space of four hundred square feet, the size of a twelve-by-twelve room, or less. Large families coped with crowded, cramped, and insufficient living space: 72 percent had no indoor toilets, and 33 percent depended on a kitchen stove or a home-built iron stove to heat their homes. The study revealed that 38 percent had no running water, 37 percent had no electric light, and 24 percent had major fire hazards, including many condemned chimneys. Almost a quarter of the families hauled their untested water directly from rivers and lakes. Outside Edmonton and Calgary, the housing situation was far worse. No wonder Métis families and individuals were moving to the cities in record numbers.

And what did they find when they arrived? The CMHC estimated that between five and ten thousand Native people were living in sub-standard housing in Edmonton.

The same thing was happening in other Canadian cities, and in the spirit of the times, the Métis and First Nations leaders began to speak out forcefully for change. Around this time, my cousin Tony Belcourt, also raised at Lac Ste. Anne, began working on housing policy as the president of the Native Council of Canada. He and his colleagues found allies for reform within the federal government after Bob Andras became the urban affairs minister. A reformer, Walter Rudnicki, became the executive director of the CMHC. He was a wonderful, caring person. I have to give credit to that man. He is the one who helped improve housing for Native people across Canada. We should honour him for that, but how many Canadians think of him today? He was eager to do something practical for Native people in a new and respectful way at a time when his help was needed most. "Housing conditions for Métis and non-status Indians were terrible," he told David Holehouse in an interview about the beginnings of Canative Housing. "There were families living in homes with no door—there could be a canvas hanging in the doorframe. There were families living in houses with no insulation, or just living in tents. It was not unusual to see people living in tents, and many times the provinces would tear them down and chase the families away."

The CMHC quickly organized an emergency repair program and a winter warmth program, but Rudnicki wanted to do something more. He appointed a man with tremendous vision, Gene Rheaume, to lead a national task force on a quest across the country for better housing solutions for Métis people. Gene had served as a Conservative Member of Parliament for the Western Arctic, and he knew how to deal with governments. He was quick on his feet and could deliver speeches, and he was liked by the Native people because he was Métis himself. His father had been a Hudson's Bay Company factor in Fort Norman, NWT; his mother traced her Scottish and Ojibway roots to the well-known Ballantyne family in Winnipeg. Their family had moved to Grouard, Alberta, so Gene grew up with a detailed knowledge of the Métis in Alberta. He had been an executive director of the Conservative Party and a chief of staff for a former party leader, Robert Stanfield.

Rheaume gathered some of his former colleagues to

work on the national task force: Louise Hayes, a former secretary to John Diefenbaker; and Gordon Hornby, a former bush pilot in the Northwest Territories and a talented administrator. Louise was a tremendous asset. She could open doors in government, and find any kind of information for people. Gordon was completely committed to making a good idea work. These three committed Canadians crossed the country and took a close look at housing conditions of the indigenous people who lived off the reserves—in rural areas, towns, and cities. "We wanted to examine housing conditions, access to housing, barriers to decent housing," Rheaume said in an interview. "The CMHC had money available to finance these groups. We just had to identify some leaders, and give them encouragement to get something going."

Rheaume and his colleagues brought their national investigation to Edmonton in 1970. "I grew up in Alberta, and I knew a lot about Edmonton," he said. "I knew Stan Daniels, president of the Métis Association of Alberta, who was one of the first leaders I ever heard to identify housing as a major priority for Native people. He gave me a good example one time. I was with him when he picked an ad for an apartment out of the newspaper and phoned to see if it was available. It was, so we arranged to go and look at it. As soon as the landlord saw Stan, and figured out I was Métis, the apartment was no longer available. It was because I was a half-breed—we both were."

I had met Rheaume a year earlier. He was organizing a Métis assembly, more of a traditional gathering, at historic Batoche in Saskatchewan. He needed hundreds of tents for the people who would be camping there, and he had found some at the Canadian Armed Forces base in Edmonton. Somebody told him: "You should talk to Herb Belcourt in Edmonton. He's a Cree boy that's got a business with lots of trucks." He contacted me, and I organized the shipment. Belcourt Construction arranged delivery of the army tents, and my brother Gordon drove them to the Métis at Batoche—now there was a reversal of history—so Rheaume had remembered me as someone who could make good things happen.

Rheaume and his colleagues on the task force wrote a background paper for the federal government based on their early findings. They were blunt. "To the list of obstacles faced by Native people in their search for identity, dignity, and the basic essentials of life, must be added the widespread though seldom acknowledged racial discrimination against them by whites." They pointed to a severe shortage of urban housing, and a "hodgepodge of disparate, often conflicting programs that create administrative inefficiency and a frightening waste of desperately needed housing funds.

"To these shortcomings must be added the consistent failure of housing authorities to involve the Native people themselves in these programs. Until recently, the involvement of Native people in their own affairs was seldom considered necessary, and the history of these special housing programs reflects this attitude. This has led, we believe, to the widespread, almost universal rejection by the Native people of these programs, which they consider to be irrelevant to their real needs as they perceive them."

Rheaume later said the task force had set a goal for itself: "We wanted to help groups set up non-profit

housing operations, and we wanted to keep those separate from the provincial Métis associations, which had a
more political agenda.

"We were looking for leaders, and one person I knew
had to be there was Herb Belcourt."

PERHAPS I WAS naïve about racism as a young man.
I often didn't see it, perhaps because I didn't want to
admit its existence. When I was looking for that first
business loan in 1965, walking from bank to bank to
bank on Jasper Avenue, I was turned down at every door
except the last one. Did racism follow me like a shadow
that day? Looking back, I wonder about the possibility.
I have also experienced hurtful remarks coming my
way from Native people. As a young man working on
a northern crew, building a power line between High
Prairie and Slave Lake, I heard someone call me an
apple, an insulting term which meant "red on the outside, white on the inside." The racial insult caught me
by surprise and bothered me a lot at the time. I put it
aside. Early in my life, I took the attitude that I didn't
give a damn what people thought about me, a blue-eyed
Métis. I figured their negativity was their problem, not
mine. I tried hard to keep that attitude, no matter what
happened. Everyone appears in this world as a human
being—white, black, yellow, you name it—and we have
an obligation to regard each person as an individual. I
have met many good people in my life, and some people
who were negative about absolutely everything. The
negative people will discriminate against all kinds of
Canadians—whether their family background is Métis
or Chinese or Ukrainian or Jewish or Arab—if we let

them. I prefer to believe that Canadians, and all North Americans, are proud of the history and culture of Métis and First Nations citizens, but I also still hear some people say things like, "We give enough money to Native people," and I can tell they are bigots.

I am more realistic about racism now that I am an older person. I am also more hopeful that the good people in the world will overcome the problem, because I have the evidence that they can work together. I can thank the lessons I learned in the development of Canative Housing.

In 1970, the *Edmonton Journal* ran a series of stories about slum landlords. Native people had been moving from reserves and settlements into the city in rising numbers, looking for a place to live. Too many of the newcomers encountered a slammed door, or met a landlord who shrugged and said, "Sorry, I've already rented the place." It was a very discouraging situation. Many families were forced to rent terrible houses that should have been condemned. They had no choice.

I didn't think anything about this situation at the time, to be honest. I read the stories in the newspapers, but I suppose somewhere in the back of my mind, I was thinking that it wasn't my problem. I had my own comfortable home, my own life, and Belcourt Construction to run. However, my cousin Tony Belcourt and other Métis leaders in Alberta had been working hard to tackle the issue. They proposed the idea of a non-profit corporation that would buy houses, renovate them, and rent them to our people. One day I received a phone call asking for my help. I can't remember who made the call, but I do remember what happened next.

"Would you come to the meeting just to listen?" the caller said. He told me that a federal minister had agreed to attend, as well as a few Social Credit cabinet ministers from the provincial government. After about an hour on the phone, just to get rid of this person, I said, "Okay, I'll come."

"Good," he said. "I'll pick you up for breakfast so we can discuss the situation."

I couldn't say no then. I had to go. I went to the meeting and listened all morning. People asked the cabinet ministers some tough questions and they replied, but the conversation was going in circles and ending up nowhere. I didn't say anything. We broke for lunch. In the afternoon, I stood up and started asking my own questions. Coffee time came. An official came up to me with an invitation: "How would you like to come to Ottawa to discuss housing for Native people in Canada?"

"I would be happy to do that," I replied, "but you'll have to send me the airline ticket and pay my expenses." I did not expect to hear another word from them.

A week later, I received a call from Ottawa. "Instead of bringing you to Ottawa, we have arranged for you to go to Winnipeg, the regional office for CMHC. We will introduce you to the manager there." And so I went to Winnipeg. I met Gene Rheaume, Gordon Hornby, and Louise Hayes, three people I would get to know very well.

The task force had some innovative ideas to consider. In Chetwynd, BC, the mayor, Frank Oberle, had built new houses for the Native people in his community within the town limits, and these people bought the houses with their own sweat equity as builders. When

Oberle became a Member of Parliament, he continued to put pressure on the federal government to involve Native people with the construction of decent housing. I remember the brainstorming at the time. I met Rheaume's task force in a room with Stan Daniels and his colleagues at the Métis Association: Thelma Chalifoux, who later became a distinguished senator, Orval Belcourt, and Tony Belcourt. We were trying together to create something new in Alberta.

We decided to create a non-profit corporation in Edmonton. Rudnicki and the CMHC agreed to support the idea as a pilot project. I had no idea how much money we would need. We decided to ask the CMHC for a five million dollar loan, and we received verbal approval for that amount.

I agreed to put a committee together to form the corporation in Edmonton. When I returned from Winnipeg, I called a meeting with the help of Orval Belcourt. About thirty people crowded into the small room, and it was soon standing room only. We discussed the idea of borrowing the five million from the government. That scared the hell out of them. They said outright that there was no way they would put their signatures against that kind of money, not for anyone, even though Orval was in favour.

I believed we had to take that step. No one would come forward, so Orval and I asked his sister Elaine McIntyre and Fred L'Hirondelle to assist us with the organization. I approached Georges Brosseau, a man I respected. Our families had known one another for years. He later said he was excited by the opportunity to assist Native people in Edmonton and Calgary to get "out of what you would call slum landlord conditions into single-family residential housing." That was the beginning. Terry Nugent, a Member of Parliament at one time, had a law firm in Edmonton, and we agreed to ask for his help to form the company. I went back to my office at Belcourt Construction and asked the staff there to brainstorm with me about a name for this new corporation. Gordon, Anna, and Peter proposed Canadian Native Housing.

I didn't like that name at all. It was labelling, and I don't like labels. Yet I knew we needed a name that would let prospective tenants know that we were there to help them. The federal government seemed to like unusual names for this sort of thing, perhaps to confuse the general public! I kept thinking about it. A few days later, Gordon Lange and I were having coffee with the staff in the boardroom. "What about Canative Housing Corporation?" he said. "That's it," I replied. We had a name.

We needed houses in a hurry. After we registered the non-profit corporation, we submitted an application to the CMHC with a request for the five million dollar loan. The federal government wanted us to buy houses in specific city blocks. We refused to do this. What a disaster that would have been. "We will not start a ghetto," we said. I believe that if a family has decent shelter in a good area—a neighbourhood where children can associate with everyone in the community, rich or poor—medical costs will come down, the children's education will be better, and everybody will win. Some government people wanted us to buy high-rise apartments and fill them with Native people. These bureaucrats had no foresight, or insight into people's needs and desires, as far as I was concerned. I will say one thing, though: Gene Rheaume, Gordon Hornby, Louise Hayes, and Walter Rudnicky were tremendous people, and they knew what they were doing. I learned a lot from them.

I started to look around, with my eyes wide open, looking at Métis families and their housing from a different perspective. After all, this was the booming Alberta of the 1970s, not the Depression years of my childhood. In the months and years that followed, I went to Morinville and other communities north and west of Edmonton, just to see for myself. Some of the housing was deplorable. There were old log houses where you could see the sun shining through the mud-filled cracks, and one-room houses with six to eight kids in them. I went away from some of them with the tears just rolling down my face. I swore we would not be defeated. Poverty prompted people to move to the city because there was a lot of work available all through the 1970s, but their lack of skills and education, as well as some prejudice, meant they couldn't get decent housing. They were turned down flat, or forced into homes that should have been condemned.

When we first opened our door for business, I will bet we had twenty-three hundred applicants. Yet I remember going to Ottawa on one of the earliest trips, when we were putting the plan together, to talk to MPs, senators, and senior civil servants about the idea. Some people tried to discourage us, even a man who became a good friend to me later on.

"Herb, don't go into this, because you'll fail," Senator Orville Phillips told me.

"No, we will not fail," I said.

I was determined to prove him wrong.

Canative Housing Corporation was incorporated in Alberta on July 22, 1971. We would triumph in ways that the senator could never have imagined, but the going was rough at the beginning. Politics complicates everything.

PETER LOUGHEED BECAME the premier of Alberta in 1971. As a strong Conservative, I welcomed the arrival of a new government and a young premier after many decades of the Social Credit administration. I also knew we would need the support of this government to get Canative Housing off the ground.

We could have taken 100 percent financing from the CMHC under the rules, but we decided to raise 5 percent of our own money. I didn't want to be completely under the thumb of the CMHC. We needed the partnership of the Alberta Housing Corporation. I asked the Lougheed government for a grant, and I was turned down flat. I didn't know what to do, so I went to see Ivor Dent, the mayor of Edmonton, and asked for his advice. He told me Alberta's mayors and other leaders had been invited to a dinner to meet the newly elected premier and cabinet. He wondered if I could attend the session and explain the situation. Ivor told me to contact Rod Sykes, then the mayor of Calgary, who was organizing the event. "Herb, I will help you and it will be a pleasure," Sykes said on the phone, "but you will have to buy some houses for Métis people here in Calgary." I would have been a fool to say no, and from that day forward we were very well acquainted.

The problem with the dinner at the Chateau Lacombe

Hotel was that only professional people were allowed to go. I didn't fit the category. I asked Georges Brosseau to represent Canative Housing at the event, because he was a lawyer. Ivor told me to wrap up a blank piece of paper and tie it with a red ribbon. The mayor presented it to Georges at the dinner, as a kind of award for providing decent housing to Native people in urban areas of the province. Then Ivor happened to mention that the request for a provincial loan had been rejected—he said loan, not grant. People questioned Peter Lougheed about why he wasn't funding the project.

The story was on the front page of the *Edmonton Journal* the next day. At 7 AM, Peter Lougheed was on the phone to me, and I could imagine his face as I listened to his voice. He was jumping two feet off the ground. He was just fuming.

"I want to see you in my office immediately!" he said.

"I'll be there at nine o'clock," I replied.

I went into his office—he had a soundproof room there, a very nice office—and he pointed his finger at me. "Don't you ever use the hammer on me again!"

"Peter, I asked you for a grant, but I'm asking you for a loan now, 5 percent of five million dollars," I said. "I'm not dishonest. I'm trying to do something for Native people in this bloody city." I hammered right back at him. I have never been afraid to go to the top with a problem, always to the top, because the person in charge will pick up the phone and call someone else, and say, "You see this person." When the boss phones, people will listen.

Within two or three days, the province approved the loan. We paid that loan back within five years. Although we had asked for five million dollars, we only used three million, and returned two million to the provincial treasury. House prices rose and we decided not to buy anything that cost more than twenty-five thousand dollars so that we could keep rents low. For a time, we took a break from buying more houses.

WE ENCOUNTERED OTHER problems in the early years of Canative Housing that led to years of public controversy, expensive lawsuits, and some painful times for me.

The corporation was a non-profit company, and the bylaws clearly stated that the company was not formed for the purpose of gain, and that no profits would be paid out to shareholders. If we dissolved the company, its assets would be transferred to a recognized charitable organization. We agreed our goal was to "establish and maintain residential accommodation for residents of the Province of Alberta of Indian ancestry, provided such residents shall be persons of low income consistent with the meaning . . . as defined in Section Two of the National Housing Act." These were the promises we made, and we kept them—whether our critics believed us or not. The proof is in the pudding.

Stan Daniels was a colourful speaker and an interesting man, the outspoken president of the Métis Association of Alberta in the 1970s. He worked hard to motivate the Native people of Alberta to assert themselves and to stand up to racism in the province, but he didn't trust me or my colleagues. We were about to submit our application to the CMHC for the five million dollar loan when we learned about a competing bid. Stan Daniels worked on this bid with a group of Alberta Métis leaders that included Joe Blyan, Freida Turcotte, and Thelma Chalifoux. The second bid created confusion at CMHC headquarters in Ottawa. Gene Rheaume, and members of the task force, phoned me with the obvious question: What are we going to do now?

We talked about it, and Gene suggested that I appoint these newcomers to the Canative board of directors. Everyone was quite happy with this arrangement. Stan Daniels discarded the application, and we began to work on our plan with about fifteen thousand dollars in federal seed money. All ten members of the first board of directors had Métis ancestry. I was the president, Clarence Longmore was vice-president, Pat Anderson was secretary, and Georges Brosseau was the treasurer. The other board members were Orval Belcourt, Fred L'Hirondelle, Joe Blyan, Freida Turcotte, Jack Johnson, and Stan Daniels. This big board—there were ten of us—became unwieldy. "We have got to dissolve this board and get rid of some of the appointed people," I told the original shareholders. I invited Stan Daniels and Joe Blyan to lunch to talk over the situation—what it was costing, the whole thing—and I asked them to make a motion to remove three board members. They did this. I had a strong desire to run Canative Housing as a business, not a political organization. Later, my colleagues and I removed Stan Daniels and Joe Blyan from the board, and they naturally resented it. That was the underlying problem, but not the only one.

Stan suspected that we would be earning an exorbitant profit on the backs of the tenants. The government had funded Native organizations up until that time; none had been run this way as a business. It came down to a matter of trust, and some of these Métis leaders in Alberta didn't trust us. Some thought we were going to make millions on the rents of the Native people, and keep it for ourselves. That was not true—then or now— but that is what they thought at the time. To win support in the community for this position, certain political leaders appealed to the bureaucrats, the government, and got them to go after us. They tried everything. They appealed to the federal government to audit our books, and they contacted the media with serious allegations of misconduct. If a tenant became unhappy with Canative Housing—with good reason, or without good reason— the story would always go to the newspapers. It was a terrible time.

Looking back, I can see they thought they were doing the right thing at the time, criticizing what we were doing. They did not see the same bigger picture we had been looking at. Yet because of them, we became more determined not to fail.

We bought more houses, renovated them, and rented them. People began to picket us, Native people, and some made wild accusations about me, the rich man "in the silk suit." More people began to think I was making a fortune from the rents of the tenants. Little did they know, my partners and I were not making anything personally on the success of Canative. I had my construction company and other businesses going, and everything we earned at Canative went back into the corporation. I absolutely did not exploit this situation, and neither did my two colleagues and business partners, Georges and Orval. We opened our books to the federal government, and we kept perfect records. To this day, we could tell you who lived in the first house, how many children were in the family, the total house cost—every nail was accounted for in our books. We ran a strict ship. When tenants were late with the rent, we would send an eviction notice on the fifth of the month. If they came to us and explained why they were behind and when they would pay, we would give them an extension. We helped many tenants by helping them arrange payments of other bills, but we expected them to pay. I may have sounded like a hard man in those days, but I did try to help people. Our rents were always in the middle of the road. If the going rent in the city happened to be $800, we would charge $650. We wanted to help the tenants become self-sufficient, to make their own way, with our help, but without relying on total handouts. In the end, it worked.

I LOOK BACK at the early years of Canative Housing with mixed feelings of pride and frustration. There were horrible days when we felt we would have to give up. For years, listening to the accusations against us in Alberta, the federal government seemed to think we were going to take the money and run.

They had created the problem, although they would not admit it. The civil servants were asleep at the switch when they put together the funding for our housing proposal. I believe the Housing Act had about eighty subsections. I knew that legislation backward and forward at one time. Federal officials combined these acts—Section 5 and Section 15, I think—to create this new non-profit organization, this experiment called Canative Housing. The original wording allowed the shareholders to transform Canative into a profit-making corporation under the Companies Act. This was probably their over-sight, made in error, but the wording clearly allowed it. Soon enough, the bureaucrats at CMHC realized they did not have full control of the money they had loaned us. They knew it, and they didn't like it. They didn't trust us, because they believed we could have made a mint, and there was not a damn thing they could do about it. If we had intended to stoop that low, we could have done it—but we never intended to exploit the situation for our own benefit.

We began to lose our allies in Ottawa. Walter Rudnicki was pushed out of the government in a highly publicized political controversy; he would later win a wrongful dismissal case. The CMHC demanded in 1974 that we reincorporate under the Societies Act. They argued that the change would eliminate any possibility of the profits going to the company's five shareholders—me, Orval Belcourt, Georges Brosseau, Elaine McIntyre, and Stan Daniels—and would open company records to public scrutiny. They also said they wanted tenants to serve on the board of directors. This sounded reasonable to the public. Many Albertans could not understand our resentment of the CMHC's ultimatums and its refusal to negotiate. We believed that non-profit corporations run by non-Aboriginal Canadians operated under the same section of the Housing Act as Canative did—but we were the ones they suspected of padding our back pockets.

At times the criticism hurt. But I knew it didn't come from anything real. In the years that followed, the federal government sued the three remaining shareholders of Canative Housing—Georges, Orval, and me—and took us to court several times. We spent a lot of money on legal fees, something between eighty thousand and one hundred thousand dollars, and so did they.

Every time the case went to a judge, the judge would rule in our favour, and finally CMHC stopped and everything was fine. The dispute was fairly straightforward. We wanted to pay off the three million dollar loan and they wouldn't accept the money. We had been paying back the loan in regular instalments, twenty-five thousand dollars a month. We owed them about $1.7 million at the time of the lawsuit, and we wanted to pay it out, but they wouldn't accept it. Now that's discrimination.

We were running Canative like a regular business, as we had promised. We made a commitment for thirty-five-year mortgages. Our interest rates were 7 percent and 8 percent. We had put away money. This was our contention: we were making money; we could pay off the loan. But you see, we weren't supposed to be making money under their guidelines, and we weren't supposed to be saving it, either. We were supposed to spend the profits every year, not have a penny left. So we created cubby holes—replacement of lawns, replacement of fences, replacement of stoves—and that's how we got around the system. We carried our own insurance policies. We bought outside policies for public liability. At the time, our insurance cost would have been twenty thousand dollars a year if we had insured the houses through an insurance company. We put away one hundred thousand dollars for self-insurance, and the CMHC people did not like that at all.

As I mentioned, Georges Brosseau, Orval Belcourt, and I ended up as the three shareholders. Gordon Hornby left Canative Housing after fifteen years of dedicated service as our manager. I had been president and treasurer through these years, but when Gordon left, Orval took over as president. I remained treasurer and also became CEO of the corporation, and I kept that position right to the very end. I took over the running of the office, overseeing the house renovations, purchasing and selling of houses, dealing with governments, and helping tenants.

I loved the work, as did my partners, but over time the disputes with government wore the three of us down. At one point, we withheld a payment from Ottawa and threatened to close the company down. Looking back, there were a few times when Georges, Orval, and I wanted to throw our hands up in the air and surrender. We didn't need this hassle. Once, when I was in Australia with my family, Georges phoned to request that I return. "They've called a public meeting and they want us there."

"Georges, why should I fly all the way back from Sydney, Australia, to attend a meeting like that in Edmonton? You are a lawyer. Stand up and tell them to go to hell." He attended the meeting and he did what he had to do. I am proud of him for that.

Every time I wanted to give up, I thought of my friend in Ottawa, Senator Phillips, saying, "You will fail." I would say to myself: "No bloody way!" And we would continue.

We exported the Canative Housing idea to other parts of Canada. Working with Gene Rheaume, Gordon Hornby, and Louise Hayes, I helped to set up other housing corporations in Nova Scotia, Ontario, New Brunswick, British Columbia, and Saskatchewan. I became the president of the Native Urban Housing

Association of Canada. My vision was to create a national housing corporation—strictly to meet the needs of Native people, and run by Native people—with a strong budget under our control. That way we could take care of our own, and take it out of the hands of the CMHC. The idea never materialized. Instead, new housing agencies emerged in the provinces on the subsidy model. I encouraged the Métis Association of Alberta, now known as the Métis Nation of Alberta, to begin a new program, called Métis Urban Housing. It eventually purchased and rented about nine hundred houses across the province. The First Nations started Amisk Housing Association in Edmonton with about ninety homes.

WATCHING THESE DEVELOPMENTS in 2003, Georges, Orval, and I decided that we were needed somewhere else. It was in education. We agreed that we wanted to invest in the future of young people. We decided to close Canative Housing and give the tenants six months' notice. They had an opportunity to buy their houses, and we helped them to arrange their financing. We transferred the assets to another non-profit corporation to finance scholarships for Métis students, the Belcourt Brosseau Métis Awards, and to give large endowments for scholarships to Edmonton's post-secondary universities and colleges. We have donated a house for Métis students and provided $500,000 over a decade, with an extra $50,000 for scholarships, to the University of Alberta; $150,000 to Athabasca University, with $50,000 for scholarships; $100,000 to NorQuest College, Grant MacEwan College, and the Northern Alberta Institute of Technology, with $25,000 for scholarships. We registered the Belcourt Brosseau Métis Awards as a corporation, and transferred Canative assets to the Edmonton Community Foundation, which invests and administers the fund. Then we approached the Alberta government with a request that it match the fund. The province contributed $1 million, but we remain hopeful that it will increase its contribution in the years ahead. The Belcourt Brosseau Métis Awards fund now stands at $14 million, and it will grow. Hundreds of young people are already pursuing their dreams with its help.

I feel so good inside that we were successful. I wanted to show people that you can do anything if you keep a positive attitude. Bureaucrats tried to kill me a few times—or put me in my place—but today we get along fine. Sometimes I meet them and we reminisce with no hard feelings. For all the criticism from the CMHC and the Native people long ago, I have seen a complete turnaround in the last five years. The Métis people have honoured me in so many different ways. It makes me feel good, and I am so very proud of them and all of their accomplishments.

I hope that all of the Canative tenants of the past will feel proud that their rent money is helping students today. They built a strong foundation for the future of the Métis people.

CHAPTER NINE

The Request

A MÉTIS WOMAN CALLED ME FROM Winnipeg. I didn't know her, I didn't know her relatives, I didn't know anything about her. She said her sixteen-year-old daughter had come to Edmonton and started hanging around with a bad crowd. She wanted her to come home.

I went around town and found that girl. I took her down to the Greyhound bus station, and bought her a one-way ticket to Winnipeg and some sandwiches and cold drinks for the trip. I sent her home to Manitoba.

"You'll never see your bus ticket money again," a staff member at the Canative Housing office told me. We laughed about it.

A few weeks later, I received a second telephone call from the girl's mother. Her daughter had left home again for Edmonton.

"Would you go and find her one more time?" she asked.

I went out again, and I found her. I took her down

to the Greyhound bus station again, bought a one-way ticket to Winnipeg again, and purchased more sandwiches and cold drinks for her trip to Manitoba. This time I spoke to her in a firm voice: "I don't ever want to see you in this city again." I meant every word of it, and she knew it.

A few months later, a middle-aged woman walked into my office. I remember that she was blind, and holding a white cane, and I had no idea who she might be. She walked up to my desk and handed me the cash to pay for two bus tickets from Edmonton to Winnipeg.

It was the girl's mother. She and her husband, an electrician, were driving across the Prairies with their children for a holiday on the west coast. The girl was travelling with them, happily. They stopped to pay a debt to a stranger, because they knew it was the right thing to do. Deep down I felt good. I hope that girl is still on the right track.

This is a story about how we care about one another.

CHAPTER TEN

An Albertan Looks at Politics

I WAS SO AFRAID TO FAIL in the early days. I believed
strongly that if I failed, people would perceive that
all Native people had failed. This attitude was probably
not fair to me, or to anyone else, but that is how I felt.

I ran for political office many times and never won
a race, but I do not regret these failures. Each lost race
taught me something, and introduced me to interesting
strangers I might not have met if I had not attempted
the challenge.

Sometimes I ran for office out of pure frustration with
the status quo. Over the years, at every election for the
presidency of the Métis Association of Alberta, Canative
Housing became the political football for the candidates.
I was tired of it. One year, I said: "I'm going to run. I'm
going to get rid of Stan Daniels!" I wanted to improve
the voting system, too, to make it more democratic. The
voting that year happened at the annual Métis assembly in Athabasca. I refused to buy votes with beer, as

1974 MAA ELECTION RESULTS

Stan Daniels pulled ahead of me in our race for the
leadership of the Métis Association of Alberta.

political candidates in all corners of the world have been
inclined to do. Even so, I came close—very, very close—
to winning. The local Native newspaper ran a humorous
cartoon about that election. The cartoonist put me in my
motorhome and my opponent, Stan Daniels, in a Métis
Red River cart as we raced to the finish line. Stan is just
a nose ahead of me in the picture when my tires deflate
with a "ssshhh . . ." I liked that cartoon. I didn't take the
defeat personally.

I entered federal and provincial politics for more
positive reasons. I had ideas I wanted to share with
people, and I had goals of my own. I wanted to see
better housing across the country for Canadians: more
affordable and better quality homes, available to all of
the people who needed a good place to live but could not
pay for one. I wanted the Métis, all of us, to feel proud
of ourselves, to get over negativity and defensiveness. I
wanted Canadians to recognize the historic contributions

of the Métis to this country. I thought that if I were in Parliament, I might be able to make a small change for the better.

Once again, I suppose I have to say that I failed to win a nomination, or win an election, and yet I won valuable insights along the way. I have had an opportunity, through my business and volunteer work, to meet many Canadian leaders. I have respected quite a few of them, and learned something different from each one.

I admired the former Conservative prime minister John Diefenbaker, because he never gave up on his aspirations, although he, too, lost many political contests before he won a race. I remember meeting him at the restaurant in the Parliament Buildings in Ottawa. He invited me to join him for lunch, and he said: "You remind me of myself when I was your age. You stand tall, proud." I have never forgotten those words. Like other Canadians, I was astonished at the man's ability to remember names years after a brief encounter, and I mentioned that to him. "You will remember that I asked you questions about yourself," he said with a laugh. "It helps that I have a photographic memory."

I respected Peter Lougheed, too. He handled himself with self-assurance when he was under pressure, and he had an ability to speak to people in a direct and forceful way. I joined the provincial Progressive Conservatives as a party member in 1969, before the party formed a government. These were the last days of the Social Credit period in Alberta. I was one of Lougheed's early supporters, because I felt the Social Credit government had been in office far too long. They became complacent and thought they were untouchable. They couldn't see the forest for the trees. They lost touch with people. When Lougheed came along, the "Now!" campaign signs went up. It was an exciting time, with change in the air. The Conservatives wanted me to run in Sherwood Park, or in the Slave Lake and High Prairie area, because I had worked in the region. Both constituencies had a high Native population, and I knew many people there. I thought about the requests both times, but I declined the invitation. I had a business to run at the time. I did fly to High Prairie to attend the nomination meeting. Larry Shaben was the candidate, and he won. Later, I helped the party with a lot of my time and energy in other areas of the province and in my home community.

I ran for the federal Conservative nomination in Edmonton–Strathcona in 1977. I had been a member of the federal party since 1958. I partly did it to help build the party. Of course, I also hoped to win. My business was doing well and I had a dedicated staff working for me, and so I became interested in the race in Edmonton–Strathcona. The other candidates were Dave Kilgour; Terry Nugent, a former MP; and Al Squair, a home builder from Sherwood Park. This was early in my marriage to my second wife, Lesley. My campaign manager and I wore out several pairs of shoes in that campaign! Other Tories were so sure I was going to win the nomination, they invited me to Ottawa to sit in the Tory caucus meeting for an orientation. I have a picture of myself in Ottawa with Joe Clark and Elmer MacKay, and I certainly hoped to win.

That was quite the nomination meeting. Al Squair bought dinner for all his supporters at a hotel, and he delivered everybody down to the party meeting at the

I met the Conservative caucus in Ottawa when I contested an Edmonton nomination in 1977. Elmer MacKay, Steve Paproski, and Ray Hnatyshyn are in the foreground, with Joe Clark seated at the table behind.

Bonnie Doon High School half an hour before the doors opened. The crowd jammed the entrance. My people couldn't get in, nor could Lesley and I enter the hall. There were two gymnasiums and they were packed, and more people were waiting outside the building than were waiting inside. The organizers called the fire department. I had to bang on the back door to get in, because the fire department had closed it. What a night! I believe it was 1:30 AM before I was finally defeated. David Kilgour won the nomination.

At the time, I was disappointed, although I did not show it. I realized people had reached their own decision, for their own reasons, but I should never have lost that nomination, because my committee sold more than three thousand memberships. The experience just made me more determined. I became president of the Pembina

Joe Clark deserved a longer term as prime minister.

Progressive Conservative Association in Sherwood Park, and I was president when Peter Elzinga ran for the federal seat and won.

I was an early supporter of Ralph Klein's leadership in the early 1990s. I thought he was more of a "people person" than any leader we had had before. Lougheed was a well-educated man, good for the province at the time, and Don Getty worked hard, but I thought Alberta needed someone different who could relate easily to ordinary people. I thought he was the person for it. I had met him when he was the mayor of Calgary, but got to know him better when he came to Edmonton and served as the environment minister.

I worked hard on his leadership campaign in 1993, selling party memberships. First we were in Calgary and he lost to Nancy MacBeth by one vote. After that there was a runoff campaign, and the other candidates gradually dropped off, until it was only Nancy and Ralph remaining in the race. Our team's job was to try to convince the other candidates to come to Ralph. I was supposed to contact the former provincial treasurer, Dick Johnson, because I knew him and his wife very well, and I knew Johnson's wife was helping Nancy. I tried to convince them to come to us. So on the Sunday after I returned from Calgary from that first nomination vote, I called Dick at his home. He promised to call me back, and did.

"No, Herb, we've decided we're going to go with Nancy," he said.

"I think you're making a big mistake," I said. "She's not going to make it." I just had that feeling somehow. I contacted Peter, Ralph, and Marvin, and they said all of the other candidates had dropped off and gone to Nancy, and they also knew about Johnson's team.

"Well," I said, "we're just going to have to step out and sell more memberships."

On Monday morning, I went to my office and started phoning every person I could possibly think of. That week I sold five hundred memberships for Ralph Klein. It was a landslide. I remember as the count came in at the

Agricom from all of these different constituencies, Ralph was sitting behind me. He grabbed my shoulders and squeezed. He was a happy man! I always liked him and his wife, Colleen, very much. Whenever I wanted to talk to him, when he was premier, the door was always open. He was always friendly. These things count with me.

As for my own political career, I ran several times but I was always defeated. I don't know if it was my background or my lack of formal education or what it was that did it. I would be considered a front-runner at the beginning of the race, and I could sell memberships with no problem. When you sell memberships, generally half of the people will come out and support you at a nomination meeting, and the other half stay home. That's the trend. But each time I ran, there was always a gang-up on me because I would always be the person to defeat. For all the defeats, I made many friends in the governments, both federal and provincial. Today I can pick up the phone and speak to just about any one of them, especially the older ones who have been in office for a couple of terms.

I might be a Conservative Albertan, but I admired Pierre Trudeau for repatriating the Canadian Constitution and insisting on a Charter of Rights and Freedoms. I also liked John Turner, because he was a relaxed, down-to-earth person in private.

I have spent a fair amount of time with Joe Clark, another former prime minister and an Albertan who made a positive impression on me. When he ran for the Conservative leadership as a young man, I supported him right to the end. We once found ourselves in deep conversation at an airport, when Joe looked out the

British Columbia MP Frank Oberle Sr., an immigrant from
Germany and a former mayor of Prince George, was a strong
advocate for better housing for Métis people.

window and saw our plane pulling away from the termi-
nal. He made a call and the plane waited—the only time
that has happened in my life—and we rushed to make the
flight. I have always found him to be a likeable person,
a very intelligent and sincere man. It is too bad he was
prime minister for such a short time. I think if he had
stayed on, Canada would have benefited.

It is important, I think, to see every person as an individual and not to dismiss political opponents altogether
because of their convictions or party affiliations. Reg
Baskin is a New Democrat organizer in Alberta, and a
union man, but like me, he used to build power lines
for a living. We became friends when we were linemen.
Once in the 1970s, when I was chairing a Chamber of
Commerce discussion, he walked into the room and sat

in the front row. I went away from the text for a second, and said to loud applause that unions were a hindrance to productivity. I was saying it as a joke, of course, because I was teasing Reg, and he just slid down in his chair and didn't say a word. However, he had a colleague at the back of the room, a young man with a beard, who decided I was the enemy. Well, you might think I had shoved a poker up that man's backside! He jumped up and he was fuming. A few days later, I was going to Ottawa and found myself sitting beside Reg Baskin and this young colleague. "What company are you going to screw up today?" I asked them. As it turned out, they were going to London, Ontario, to try to unionize a bank, so I had hit the nail right on the head. Reg and I chatted all the way, but his colleague wouldn't speak to me. When we reached our destination, Reg turned to his friend and said: "Can't you see he is just pulling the chain on you real tight? He is joking." Reg understood me. I think people have to work on listening to people, and recognizing their honesty, even when they disagree. Reg and I could always do that, although we stand on opposite sides of the political spectrum.

I have known Preston Manning for many years, ever since he was a young man. One day we were sitting together, having a coffee, when he said, "Herb, I'm going to start a new party. Would you help me?" I did not have to think over his request. "I think you're a great man, Preston, and I admire you for wanting change," I said. "I don't believe in some of your right-wing views, so I have to decline your invitation for help." We left it at that. Later I received an invitation from the Reform Party to stand for election to the Canadian Senate. (At the time, Alberta was experimenting with an election process, even though the federal government appoints Canadians to the Senate.) Again, I had to turn them down. I had nothing against them as people, but their policies are not for me.

Some people detest politicians and dislike the backroom politics and compromises that seem to bend everything out of shape. I have always been interested in politics as a way of finding out what is happening in my country, in my province, and in my community. I enjoy talking with politicians. Sometimes I tell them they have lost touch with reality. I have never been afraid to tell them what I think, because I believe most people value an honest opinion.

Not all of my opinions fit perfectly within a Conservative party platform. For example, I am disappointed that our natural resources in Alberta—our rich supplies of oil and gas—are tied up with the North American Free Trade Agreement. We have all the oil here in Alberta, yet as Canadians we have to pay world prices. I don't think we can continue relying on oil. We have to look at other sources of energy. The federal government is reaching too many agreements that harm Canadians as it continues to bend to the influence of the United States. The American government is like Big Daddy. What will they want next? Our water? I would like to see our leaders stand up and tell the United States government when enough is enough. Alberta has become too American in its perspective. Large US corporations control our lives, from stores to television. They are influencing our political leaders. We have seen the uproar in Alberta about privatized health care. If Canadians have one thing we

I would not vote for Jean Chretien's party, but I admired the Liberals' patriation of the Canadian Constitution, and creation of the Charter of Rights and Freedoms.

need to fight for, it is the survival of our medical system. Yes, we must work to improve it, but we must not destroy the system in our efforts to bring positive change.

We are sending more troops to Afghanistan, and I am worried about the consequences. I think Canadian soldiers should remain in a peacekeeping role, but now the federal government is asking us to accept that this country is at war. This is wrong, in my view, because the new role does not fit with our view of ourselves as Canadians.

I would like to see travel subsidized so more Canadians could get to know one another, and to appreciate their country in new ways. I would like Canada to adopt the best ideas of other nations; in Ireland, for example, the country is prosperous and proud, and offers free transportation and telephone service to many seniors. We could learn more from other countries than we do.

I want the Alberta government and the federal government in Ottawa to do more to protect our environment. I would like to see more Métis and First Nations people in the House of Commons and Senate, and in every provincial government in the country. Albertans have elected Mike Cardinal, Pearl Calahasen, and Denis Ducharme, but our legislature would be well served with more Native representatives. And even though I was very proud when former prime minister Brian Mulroney invited me to attend a dinner in Winnipeg with the Queen, I would like to see a Canadian citizen serve as the ceremonial head of state. It would be such an honour for a Native person to serve in that role, such a powerful symbol of respect for the first peoples of this land after everything that has happened in our history.

Every citizen could talk about dreams for a better Canada, and I suppose we will never agree on all of them. I think it is important to dream, take action when we can, and never wait for other people to do it for us.

The Métis people in Alberta are fortunate to have strong leaders, a tradition that goes back to our earliest days in the western territory. Some of them have worked to build political organizations, while others devoted their energy to community work.

I admired Stan Daniels for his hard work for all Native people in Canada, although, as I have said, the two of us had our differences over the years. Older people will remember his strong and spirited way of protesting injustices. When he wanted to protest the high price of food in northern communities, he carried a sausage all the way from northern Alberta to Ottawa. He had been charged $2.90 a pound for garlic sausage—a price any Canadian at the time would find ridiculous—but he used the trip to talk about the wider needs of northerners. He started the Winter Works program, repairing the windows and doors of Native families' homes in northern Alberta. That program—and many others he envisioned—made life better for the Métis people.

Jim Sinclair was one hell of a man. A fighter. He fought for the rights of Native people in Saskatchewan. Jim received the lifetime achievement award at the National Aboriginal Achievement Awards on the night I received the award for my work in housing. He was the type of person who would never give up. He was instrumental in starting the Back to Batoche Days, where I first met him. He was the one who requested the tents that my brother Gordon took to Batoche. He would always call on people in Ottawa to help him achieve what he wanted to do.

When Larry Desmeules became the president of the Métis Association of Alberta, he started the Native Urban Housing Association and Apeetogosan, an economic development agency and lending office for emerging businesses. We spent many hours discussing Native politics at his home. His wife, Anne, made a lot of tea for us while we changed the world at the kitchen table. We talked about banking and discussed ways that the Métis Association might start its own bank in Alberta. He wanted to have Métis identification cards made for people to increase pride in our identity. I thought he had good vision.

Stan Daniels

Audrey Poitras has been an excellent leader for the Métis Nation of Alberta. She is the first woman to serve as president. She carried on some of the work that Larry Desmeules had started before his death—to help to create new businesses, and to encourage Métis people to be independent and self-sufficient—but she also had vision of her own. She created Métis Crossing, a heritage site that will educate the young and old about Métis history and lifestyle. This site is located south of Smoky Lake, and I know it will attract tourists. Our vision is that schools could take students there by bus, travel by voyageur canoe from the Métis Crossing Centre to an outdoor area where they could enjoy a fish fry-up, then return to the centre on a Métis Red River cart. A platform will be built high up in the trees, and I expect children will enjoy that, too. I am excited about Audrey's

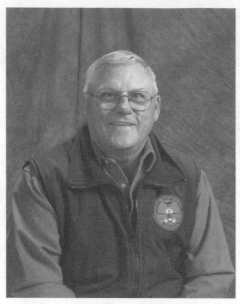

Chester Cunningham
PHOTO COURTESY OF THE ABORIGINAL MULTI-MEDIA SOCIETY OF ALBERTA

plans for this important celebration of our culture. In her quiet way, Audrey gets things done. She has surrounded herself with good people. This shows leadership.

Thelma Chalifoux has a great knowledge of Métis history, and she has returned to Alberta to run the Michif Cultural and Resources Institute in St. Albert. I admire her for her direct way of speaking to people. She is not afraid to say what she thinks. I can see why she became a Canadian senator. I first knew her when she worked for the radio station in Peace River. When I was involved in Native organizations, Thelma was always working nearby. She has had a positive influence on our lives as Métis people.

Some of the most effective leaders in Alberta prefer to work behind the scenes in the community, away from the storms of political life. In 1970, Chester Cunningham recognized an urgent need to assist those Native people in the courts who could not afford representation. He told me he even put a mortgage on his house so he could afford to represent them. He created Native Counselling Services of Alberta, and also worked hard to establish the Stan Daniels Centre, a minimum-security centre for offenders in Edmonton. Chester was honoured with the Order of Canada for his excellent work. I respected the way he kept political dissension out of his organization. His service to the Métis people of Alberta will never be forgotten.

When Chester retired from Native Counselling Services, his successor, Al Benson, carried on his dream. Al created Cunningham Place so that Native people with addiction problems could find more shelter and counselling. Al is committed to a goal of carrying on Chester's dream. Well respected by business people in Edmonton, he has been honoured by the Rotary Club. He has increased the staff of Native Counselling Services to more than 150 people, and he treats his staff well. He praises and encourages them. If a family member of one of his staff has a problem or illness, Al will immediately direct his supervisors to help. He brings out the best in people, which makes him an excellent leader. Al is involved in the World Conference on Poverty, and he works closely with the Edmonton Police Service to improve the treatment of homeless people in our city.

All of these people have contributed their gifts to our society. I have been grateful for their service, and for their friendship.

Some of the most satisfying work I have done in my life has been in the volunteer sector. I have served on the boards of large and small community organizations, including the Board of Governors for Athabasca University, Native Counselling Services, and the Commanding Officer's Aboriginal Elders Advisory Committee of the RCMP, K Division. I have also served on the boards of Safe Place, the Strathcona women's shelter; the Inner City Church Corporation; and the Strathcona Care Foundation. I have tried to encourage more Native people to enter business through my work on the boards of Apeetogosan (Métis) Development Inc., Native Venture Capital Corporation, the Business Assistance for Native Albertans program, and the Chamber of Commerce. I have enjoyed assisting arts organizations as a board member with the Alberta Foundation for the Arts, Festival Place in Sherwood Park, and other groups. Recently I worked with a strong team—a local county councillor, Linda Osinchuk, the RCMP, Parents Empowering Parents (PEP), and Strathcona Family Services—to organize the Community That Cares information evening. We hope to enlighten our community about the destructive nature of drugs such as crystal meth.

Looking back, I am glad I did not win a political party nomination or an election. It took me a long time to learn that a Canadian can be just as effective outside Parliament. You don't have to sit in a provincial legis-lature, or win a seat on city council, town council, First Nations band council, or Métis settlement council, and you don't have to become the president of an organiza-tion, in order to create change in your community. In fact, I believe that citizens can create more change on the outside, as long as they learn the way the political system works. The bureaucrats will make you or break you. Remember that.

CHAPTER ELEVEN

The Belcourts and the Fur Business

WHENEVER I WALK IN THE front door of Ken Belcourt Furs, I sense my father's presence. My family has been in the fur business since the 1700s, perhaps longer, and this tradition endured through the twentieth century and into a new millennium. When my father died, his long-time associate, Sheppe Slutker, told an *Edmonton Journal* reporter that Dad had endured many hard times as a travelling fur buyer in the north, travelling through blizzards, "and at least once, he had wrapped himself up in the furs he had bought to keep himself from freezing to death." As a young man, I chose other work because I did not believe in killing wild animals. I do recognize the importance of the fur business in Canadian history, and I appreciate that many generations of the Belcourt family have relied on furs for their livelihood. The Métis built a national economy around this work.

My brother Ken keeps the tradition alive with the

Wilfred Belcourt, my father.

help of other members of our family. His shop on 105th
Avenue in Edmonton is a doorway into a much larger
business. Through his long career, he has exported
thousands of furs from Alberta to Europe and Asia.
He is a walking encyclopedia of traditional knowledge
about trapping, fur-buying, and fur selling. My father
also trained my other brothers, Gilbert and Gordon,
and the oldest sister, Georgina, in different aspects of
the business. Preserving this knowledge is important to
me, and to the Métis people of Alberta, so I asked each
of them to talk about their experiences and their views
about the future of the industry.

KEN BELCOURT

I am the second oldest in the Belcourt family, born in
May 1933. I was twelve years old when my dad began to
train me in the fur business at our home west of Lac Ste.
Anne. Something lured me to it. When my father was

away from home on buying trips, other trappers from the Alexis reserve and the Glenevis area would come to the house with squirrels and muskrat skins to sell. I would pay them with the few dollars I had, nickels and dimes, you might say. My father gave me the money to help me learn the trade. Once I started, I didn't want to stop. I just kept going.

Our parents were hardworking people. My father was always buying fur in the wintertime; in the summer, he would buy cattle. Like Herb, I left home when I was fifteen to go to work, and then I worked as a painter. The next year, I started out on the road with my father, travelling across northern Alberta on fur-buying trips. He trained each son separately on these trips. It got better and better after that.

We had a route for each trip. We would go from Edmonton, through Smoky Lake, Villeneuve, Spedden, St. Paul, Elk Point, Cold Lake, Grand Centre, and Bonnyville, then circle back to Lac La Biche, Athabasca, Slave Lake, Valleyview, High Prairie, and Grande Prairie. From Peace River, we went north to Manning, High Level, Indian Cabins, and Fort Vermilion. We would go out to Grande Cache and the area near the mountains. We would sometimes go north to the iso-lated settlements north of Lesser Slave Lake—places like Wabasca, Trout Lake, and Peerless Lake. We went all over northern Alberta.

We would be away sometimes a week, sometimes ten days. We travelled in a pickup truck to start off with, but then we had a car and later a station wagon. We would fill the station wagon with furs, often squirrels, decking the skins like cordwood in the back of the car and on the roof. Sometimes we would tie the furs in bales, put the bales in special bags, and ship them by bus or by truck to Edmonton as we drove along our route, because there was plenty of fur wherever we went in those days.

If we went a long way into the bush to a settlement, we always came back to a town the same day, often at two or three o'clock in the morning. We would stay in hotels in Slave Lake, High Prairie, and Peace River. Each year we would go on the road toward the end of October. There was no fur to buy at that time, but we went down the road to say hello to all of our customers and to tell them we would be back to buy fur for the winter. By the second week, people would start selling fur to us. It just kept going like that, very busy all winter.

Fur was the major trade in the north at that time. Many people made their living on trapping in all of those communities, and it was the only source of income on most of the reserves. There was no such thing as welfare. The government offered a little bit of something called relief, but you had to be very sick or disabled to get it. The people all over the north were very proud people at that time—both the Native people and the northern homesteaders. They were proud of their trapping ability.

Most of the trappers were the Native people and the Métis people. The northern homesteaders had to trap, too, in order to survive, because they had no income to speak about. The homesteader was a poor man and he got some land—I don't know how he got the land from the government, but he settled on his land. He would have to trap to feed his family, the same as the Native people.

The Belcourt brothers, left to right: Gilbert, Ken, Herb, and Gordon.

The Natives always handled the fur the best. It was all raw. They skinned and dried them in such a way that you could ship those furs anywhere in the world in good condition.

When my father and I arrived in a community, we would visit the trappers. We would size and grade the furs, such as beaver, to determine the price. *Number one, number two, slight damage, damaged, and poor.* We would have a price for each grade, and this applied to all the animals the same way. The only trappers who didn't handle the furs very well were the homesteaders, perhaps because they lacked the experience.

I went out on my own on a fur-buying trip for the first time when I was seventeen years old. I could buy from anybody the first year, but then they changed the law. Travelling fur buyers like my dad and me could only buy from local dealers in the community. They were usually country storekeepers. They would grubstake the trappers in their area. That means they would supply traps and other supplies on credit. If we came along and paid cash for furs, the storekeepers wouldn't get paid. I guess there must have been a complaint to the government, so they changed the law. Under the new system, the trappers sold furs to the local storekeepers and we bought the furs from them. The middle man got a chunk of the money. The trappers didn't mind, because the storekeeper was in the area all the time and could supply them with groceries and give them credit until they brought in their furs. Some storekeepers would give the people credit all summer when there was no trapping. The trappers would start to pay off their summer bill when they went back to their traplines in the late fall. They would clear the bill up by spring. This seasonal economic system would be like a round ball. It just kept going round and round.

My father had a successful business relationship with an independent fur buyer in Edmonton, Sheppe Slutker, who operated Slutker Furs and Hide Co. Their agreement worked for both of them for many years. When we went on the road, my dad carried what they called a draft book. We could walk into any bank in northern Alberta and they would give us the cash to trade for furs. When I went on the road, I got a draft book from Mr. Slutker, too. I still have one to remind me of those years. My dad and Mr. Slutker were not business partners exactly. They were both independent. I was on my own, too. Mr. Slutker agreed to supply cash to us as an advance, so that we could make payments to trappers. We agreed to sell him the fur that we collected in the north.

The fur market, and the fur supply in Alberta,

fluctuated widely over time. In the late 1940s, we bought plenty of muskrats, then beaver, then lynx. We also bought a lot of squirrels. The Native families—the wife and the kids would go with their husbands on the traplines—would be trapping squirrels. We used to pay them fifty cents a squirrel. We made a nickel on the squirrel, but these people could trap two to three thousand squirrels, so a nickel turned into a little bit of money for all of us. When I went on the road, I used to buy enough squirrels to pay for my expenses. In those days I could pay for my gas, hotel room, and food for a hundred dollars a week. Today, that amount would not be enough for a day.

We had many adventures on the road, travelling in the north in winter. We got caught in lots of blizzards. I remember we got caught once between Grande Prairie and Beaverlodge. We ran out of gas on the road at five o'clock in the morning. The wind chill made the temperature something like minus sixty. Fortunately, somebody came along and pushed us into Beaverlodge. We found a hotel there, and once we had the gas, we were ready to go again. I can remember another time when my dad borrowed Herb's car. The radiator kept leaking. We had a cream can to fill the radiator, to keep it going when it boiled. We were coming back, around Westlock where it is all open land, and the wind was blowing the snow off the fields. It would blow the black dirt across the road, just about every year, because the wind was so strong. Anyway, the motor stopped on us at about three or four in the morning. We figured out that the strong wind was behind us. We opened the four car doors—and you may not believe this, but the wind carried us down that highway on glare ice. We opened the doors and away we went.

We had competition on those fur-buying trips. The Hudson's Bay Company had stores all over the north, and travelling buyers on the road. We couldn't buy from those people. That wasn't the law, just the regular practice, the business tradition. The Hudson's Bay Company had an auction sale in Montreal, so all their fur had to be sold there. They were our main opposition.

We were always the major buyers in northern Alberta—the Hudson's Bay Company and the Belcourts. Mr. Slutker must have had a good market. He had his connections in Winnipeg. In the spring, we would buy most of the beaver in the north, because he seemed to have a good market for it. The Hudson's Bay didn't want to compete with us in this area, so the trappers sold us the beavers in the spring.

My dad passed on his knowledge to me. By the time I went on the road with him at sixteen, I could already grade and buy fur. We had a buying system worked out. He was a good public relations person—that's what I would call him. We would go to a trapper's place. I would do all the grading, writing everything on a piece of paper, while he entertained the trapper and his wife. She would be making tea and bannock, and together they would be laughing and talking, while I graded the fur. When I finished, I gave him the grade sheet. He would put the price on the list and then buy the fur. That's the way we did it. He trained one Belcourt son at a time. When I was with him, it would be just the two of us. There were two other boys who travelled with him. Gilbert, who is a year younger than me, travelled with my dad too. Our younger brother Gordon still buys furs for me.

I learned a long time ago that you must buy fur and resell it yourself to make a profit. If you give it to somebody else to sell for you, you never make any money because they get first count. When someone else gets first count, there's nothing left for you. I've sold a lot over the years and I think it is because I learned that rule. I have sold fur all over the world for the last thirty years. I used to go to the fur auction sales, but I learned something about that, too. In my experience, if you're a fur buyer and you buy a lot of goods, you cannot give it to an auction sale to sell, because they sell to the highest bidder. That means, if you paid a hundred dollars for the fur and the highest bid is ten dollars, they sell it!

The trapping business is definitely not what it used to be. About fifteen years ago, the prices collapsed. Before that, the fur prices were high enough for a trapper to make a good living. When the prices fell, many people stopped trapping. That meant that fewer fur buyers could make a living on the profits they were earning, so they stopped going on the road. Then even fewer trappers had fur for sale. I happen to think it is still possible to buy and sell furs and make money, but many people disagree with me. Face it: it costs a hundred dollars a day to drive a vehicle all over the north, a hundred dollars for a place to sleep, and fifty dollars for meals. With fewer northerners selling furs, it is a long way between trappers, and gas costs are high.

Heavy industry in northern Alberta has had a big impact on trapping, too. Trappers have always used the oil and gas companies' cut lines and other service roads to reach their traplines, but other aspects of the oil and gas and forestry industries hurt the trapping industry. The big timber is disappearing. A lot of animals, like the squirrels, live in the big spruce trees because that's where their food is. There are still a lot of squirrels in the country, scattered all over, struggling to make a living, you might say.

We see wide changes in the supply of different animals over the years, due to the ecology of the northern bush. The main source of food for the lynx is the rabbit. Every time the rabbits multiply in great numbers, the lynx also multiply because the food source is increasing. We haven't had muskrats in any quantity in northern Alberta for thirty or forty years, for some reason. Now they're coming back, but they will not stay unless we keep the existing water or get water. The otter is moving. There used to be a lot of otter in northern Alberta—and there still are in northern Saskatchewan—but their main source of food is the beaver. They suck the blood out of them and they eat a little bit of the flesh, but not a lot. The beaver have to have the water. They need all the creeks to build dams, where they live. Years ago, when we used to get five or six feet of snow, the snow would melt, clean their water up, flood their dams, and wash all the debris away. The beaver remained healthy. That doesn't happen as much now. When they have no snow meltwater, they have to live in that dirty water. It's not good for them, or their pelts.

The anti-fur campaigners had a big impact on the Alberta trapping industry, because they went to European governments to prohibit fur sales in those countries. They opposed the leg-hold trap, which they said was cruel to the animal. That trap is outlawed now in Canada, although it can be used in water. When animals drown in the water, they die immediately and don't suffer. The trap used any other way is illegal.

The fur business has come back since the law appeared, but I think the entire trapping industry needs an overhaul. Years ago, the people went out on the traplines and stayed there in the bush by themselves. Before the northern communities had schools, the trapper took his whole family into the bush and they worked together. That's not the way it is today. The children have to go to school. The young trappers need to spend much more money on modern equipment to make a living. Their parents or grandparents—who were working back when I started—could buy a set of leg-hold traps for six or seven dollars a dozen. Today, trappers have to pay $125 to $150 for a dozen modern traps, and you can't make a living with a dozen traps. You need fifteen dozen, or something like that, and you have to have the Ski-doo. To become a trapper today, to make a living, you need to invest twenty to thirty thousand dollars in equipment.

That's big capital. Few of the young people in the north have this kind of money. Good workers can earn a lot more in the oil fields with no advance investment. They are not waiting for the fur market, worrying about prices, or anything like that. The young Native people who want to stay at home in the community—even the ones who want to live like their ancestors, as trappers—have no money to buy this equipment. Absolutely nothing. They don't have local buyers in their communities, like their grandparents did, who can supply them with equipment and supplies on credit. The old system doesn't work.

I think trapping regulations and procedures should be changed, and trapping should be run as a business. There might be a million muskrats in Alberta, and I might find a market for a million muskrats. If I found a market for half a million muskrats, we couldn't get them because the people don't have the traps to get them. Our business, or someone else with enough money, could hire the trappers. You could still have strict conservation rules. You could set up a work camp just like the oilfield work camps—a place where they could come in at night for food and shelter, with TV to watch—and they could use company equipment to trap, and company Ski-doos to get around in the bush. If the trappers also wanted to skin and stretch the furs, the company could pay them extra as an incentive. Other northerners could be hired for this task. The company could hire different people to trap, skin, and dry the furs, and to cook and clean for the crews. It would be a way to keep a historic resource industry alive in Canada, and to keep a traditional Native economy going in a new and efficient way. I don't think my idea has ever been tried, but I am hoping to develop it this year.

I am almost ready to retire. I don't go on buying trips anymore. I have to do it a different way. I can't do the physical work, but I can sell. I talk to people on the phone. I have had a request from China for two hundred thousand muskrats, and I've sold seventy thousand muskrats to another customer in England. I can't fill large orders because of the fall in production. Many trappers are not doing anything with their traplines, because the old system doesn't work anymore. That's why I want to see a change.

I was born in September 1934, the third son in the family. They say our father used to walk fifty miles when he was first buying furs. He would leave Lac Ste. Anne, go to Sangudo, Mayerthorpe, back to Gunn, and home again. He bought muskrats in those days for nickels and dimes, and carried them home on his back. Later he used a team of horses and a cutter, and after that a Model-A Ford so he could go to Edson and Marlboro and Hinton, and all the bush country in between.

I started buying furs with him in the 1940s. He didn't train us, exactly. We watched him grade furs at home. By the time we were fifteen, we knew how to do it. We would drive up to Fort Nelson, up the Mackenzie Highway. Gordon, my younger brother, went too, when he was old enough. We would drive from Mayerthorpe to Blue Ridge, Whitecourt, Fox Creek, Little Smokey River. As Ken said, Dad would talk to the dealers or the trappers. He liked to talk to people. While he talked, I would grade furs and separate them according to size and quality: *Extra and blankets. Large. Large–medium. Smalls. Kits and smalls.* We had seven different sizes of beavers, for example.

There were not that many vehicles in those days. We would buy from dealers who would grubstake the trappers. We guaranteed our dealers the fur prices in advance, and they would supply the trappers with equipment and credit. They sold food and traps. We never lost a storekeeper. Dad would buy the furs for Mr. Slutker, who owned Slutker Fur and Hide. The Hudson's Bay Company had lots of posts, and big advantages against the smaller dealers, who couldn't go into the reserves to meet Native trappers. The HBC seemed to have a claim on every skin caught in Canada, from the days of the Royal Charter in 1670 to 1979. We had to work hard. We bought from anybody, and they were all good customers, as far north as Grande Prairie and beyond, across northern Alberta and northern BC.

When the fur market would crash for one skin— beaver, say—we would concentrate on something else. Up at Jasper, Blue River, McBride, and Prince George, we picked up a lot of marten. Williams Lake. Bella Coola. For three or four years, we seemed to be on the road all the time. I used to say sometimes: "What am I doing in this country?" The driving could be very tough. There was so much snow in the mountains, narrow trails for sleighs, and road curves very sharp. I remember a blizzard at Alexis Creek. We turned around and I never went back to that country. We drove a pickup truck and a van to Prince Rupert, Watson Lake, into the Yukon. I remember one time at Watson Lake, the wind was blowing at minus fifty or sixty, a huge blizzard. We drove ahead, and four guys followed close behind so we could get through it together. It was so cold, the clutch wouldn't go. I also remember the old buying trips though Hay River, Fort Simpson, and Fort Liard. Sometimes we'd pick up a thousand marten, five hundred squirrels, all graded on the spot. We packed the skins in sacks.

There were good trappers everywhere in those days, in the 1940s and 1950s. I remember a man named Dolphus Capablank. He brought us a hundred lynx one time. He was quite a trapper, a go-getter. I knew everybody along the Alaska Highway in those days, every trapper all the way north.

The Belcourts and the fur industry belonged together. We were legends of the north, and I don't mind saying that. We were the fur buyers. We remember people involved in the business, people we knew on the road over the years. Sam Jama. Sam Will at Lac La Biche. John Ross. Alfreds' Fur and Hide.

I don't think Albertans recognize today how important the fur business was in the north country in the years before oil and gas, and forestry. We brought the cash that fed the people in all of those communities. When I go into a place like High Level, I think about that. We would bring twenty thousand dollars into High Level, in rolls of cash, in my days in the business. When the oil rush came into any area, the oil boom, the trapping would go down. Then the oil work would die down, and people went back to trapping. We fed the north in those days. The trappers' families bought their groceries on credit until we came to buy their furs, and then they paid off the shopkeepers. The storekeepers, our dealers, depended on us too. Even the farmers trapped in the north. It was an economy for the region.

I feel good about that, the Belcourt name. We did a lot to help people survive the harder times, guaranteeing the fur purchases from the dealers. We sometimes had to fly into those communities, from Peace River. We would buy from Fleury L'Hirondelle (and the trappers in the back lakes, north of Lesser Slave Lake), and fly in on a Cessna 185 to pick up fur. Sometimes we would have to go back to town for more money to pay for fur.

We didn't need to worry about travelling with that cash. We could trust people. In Fort Nelson, we went out to find the trappers. If a trapper looked Native, you didn't even ask him for a guarantee. You just knew it would be fine. I learned a little of the languages of the people along the way: Cree, Slavey, or Dene. Those families made a good living. They could walk away with five thousand dollars for a stack of a hundred marten. They would know we were coming, too, long before we got to them. Up at Steen River, there was a two-way radio. Jimmy Jones would get on and say: "Belcourt is going to be here." We would be there by nightfall. They would come in by dog team—there were still loads of trappers on dog teams in the 1950s—bringing in furs. The trappers in those days would also walk fifteen miles with stacks of furs on their backs. Those packs were so heavy. They would take turns carrying these bales of skins. I remember once we were buying at Assumption, and some trappers came in from the Rainbow Lake area. They had walked sixty or seventy miles with a hundred pounds on their back, taking turns packing it. At Fort Vermilion, it would be the same. These men worked hard.

We made a good living, travelling the road. We would stay in a small place, eat at local cafés or eat with people at their homes. One thing I want to say about Native people: If the kids trapped their own skins, even if it were lynx or marten, they kept that money. The parents didn't make them hand it over.

At Fort Nelson we bought a lot of the best beaver. Just like diamonds. Short nap, long fur. I remember a time in 1973 when Mr. Slutker and I beat the best buyer from England with a special purchase of select beaver. I turned it over for a high profit. The Belcourt boys and Mr. Slutker bought 85 percent of the furs in Alberta from 1965 to 1980.

The fur business is dying today. Nobody is buying locally, almost nobody. Only the trappers with big operations have survived. They are earning a small percentage of what they did in the good days. They have no place to sell the skins near home, and most have retired. I don't think the fur business is finished entirely, but it's a very tricky situation. There will still be buyers, but it's more complicated now. Ken is still in it. Sometimes my brother Gordon buys coyotes from the Hutterites; Belcourt Furs buys about fifteen thousand coyotes a year, about 80 percent from the Hutterites. Buyers in China wanted two hundred thousand muskrats, but it is harder to supply these foreign buyers with wild fur. Ranch fur is different. Wild fur has gone down to 10 percent of the business. Ranch fur is about 90 percent of the business. Pearl blue mink, black mink—that's the twenty-karat diamond of the business now.

GORDON BELCOURT

There was a lot of trust in the north when we started in the fur business. You could leave a pile of skins someplace, and they wouldn't be touched. The old trappers were honest. They didn't lock their cabins. We have had times when quite a lot of cash would be left behind, and then it would be found, and all the cash returned by the RCMP. The muskrats would be in the pack, and Dad would do a count, and they would all be there. We knew everybody. Dad knew hundreds, maybe thousands, of people by name all across the north. I don't know how he did that.

I think my father would have been recognized as a brilliant man if he had had an education. He had Grade Two,

I think, but he could add faster in his head than anyone could calculate on a computer. My mother was a hard worker—making bread, washing all our clothes on the old scrub boards, and keeping our family together. Mum was trying to raise the family while Dad was on the road making a living. They were strict with us, but they weren't mean.

Mr. Slutker's office was on 101st Street in Edmonton, between 103rd and 104th Avenue. Later we moved to 109th Street, where Peace Hills Trust is today. Mr. Slutker was known as the Rabbit King. My dad bought thousands of rabbits in the 1940s. He would come home looking like a snowman. During the war, they used rabbit fur to pack guns(for shipment overseas). They even used skunks. On the train, the northerners used to call the odour of skunks "the money smell."

GEORGINA BELCOURT KOSICK

I worked with my dad as a bookkeeper in his fur business. I remember one time I got a call from him. He asked me to get thirty thousand dollars out of the bank, and get on a plane.

"Go to Fort Chip," he said.

On my way to Fort Chipewyan, someone asked me if I were a newspaper reporter.

I was laughing. I was carrying the money with me to buy furs up there.

My husband and I had our own business, P.K. Construction. We shared an office with my father on 109th Street, south of Jasper Avenue, so that I could do the bookkeeping for both businesses. My father later moved downtown to 101st Street, across from City Centre, but I continued to work with him for several years.

Georgina Belcourt Kosick, my sister, worked with
my father and brothers in the fur business.

I learned various aspects of the business. My dad
graded all the furs and packed them in different boxes for
shipment to his customers. I would help him pack the furs
for shipment overseas, and for fur auctions in Winnipeg.
He had many people helping him do that. We used to ship
muskrats to Ecker Furs in England. I remember once I
travelled to Winnipeg with Dad for a fur auction.

When I was alone in the shop, trappers would come
in to sell their furs, and I bought them directly. When I
first started, I overpaid them, and I heard about it later!
My dad and brothers would laugh about it. The next
time the same people came in, I would say: "I am not so
dumb this time," and then I would pay the right price.

My father was experiencing heart trouble just before
my husband and I went away on a long trip to Asia in
1976. I made an appointment for him with the doctor.

When I returned, I asked him about it, and he said: "I don't have much time." I tried to encourage him to keep going. "Don't you want to see your first granddaughter married?" I said. A family wedding was coming up. He said: "I will try." He died that winter in Fort Chipewyan.

I am proud of whatever my family has accomplished in the fur business. My brothers knew more than I did because they were working at a very young age, but I learned a lot, too.

CHAPTER TWELVE

Saying Goodbye

MY FATHER, WILFRED, DIED OF a heart attack at Fort Chipewyan on December 4, 1976, when he was sixty-nine. He had been on a fur-buying trip in the community when his car got stuck in a snowdrift. After battling the cold and pushing the car out of the drift, he stopped at the cabin where he always stayed on his trips to Fort Chip. He gave his money and fur to the cabin owner and then went to lie down. He died right away.

I flew up there immediately with my brother Ken and my brother-in-law Peter Kosick. We took a metal casket with us, as the funeral home in Edmonton had requested. By then, my father's body had been taken to the nursing station. I was shocked to find his body lying outside on the snow behind the nursing station. His chest and stomach were bare, and I could not pull down the thin T-shirt to cover him, as it was frozen. His body was swollen almost beyond recognition.

Although the nurse said they had no suitable place to

store his body, I was distressed at the way they had disregarded my father, showing him no final respect. There were plenty of empty rooms in the nursing station, where the heat vents could have been shut off or the windows left open. Another alternative would have been to take his body to the RCMP garage. I told them so.

Later, the Edmonton undertaker, Bill Connelly, told me that this type of disregard for a dead body, and the improper handling, were common occurrences among the authorities in Native communities in Alberta. My father's body was so badly frozen that it took three days to thaw him and suitably prepare him for viewing at the funeral. I immediately wrote to then Solicitor General Roy Farran, who promised to investigate. He assured me an incident like this would not happen again.

My mother, Florence Belcourt, who was seven years younger than my father, died in a nursing home in Edmonton on November 28, 2003.

CHAPTER THIRTEEN

Joys, Sorrows, and Beautiful Children

I WOULD NEVER WANT TO LIVE alone. My wife, Lesley, our children, and our grandchildren mean everything to me. I don't know what I would do if something happened to them. When I come home and I turn down the street toward our house, I look forward to seeing everyone. I know I am a lucky man.

Like every couple, Lesley and I have shared great happiness in the past thirty-five years, and we have struggled through difficult challenges and heartbreaks. When we married, we could never have anticipated that we would be raising grandchildren when I reached my seventies. Our path through life has taken many unexpected twists and turns, but we are fortunate to be walking ahead together.

I met Lesley on an unforgettable day in 1971. She was a young, adventurous teacher from London, England, who had decided to try her luck in Canada. She taught for two years in the small Dene Tha' community of Meander

Herb, Jolene, Colin, and Lesley Belcourt.

River in northern Alberta, not far from the border of the Northwest Territories. One summer she came south to Edmonton to take education courses at the University of Alberta in order to improve her teaching credentials. I was having lunch with Stan Daniels at the King Edward Hotel when he saw her, and having met her earlier at a Métis association event, he introduced us. I thought she looked lovely that day. She still does.

I think I asked her out for coffee after work. I had been working all day and I was wearing a business suit when I picked her up. We had a good conversation, and I asked her out for dinner a few days later. Apparently, she thought to herself: "What will he wear to dinner if he meets me in a business suit for a cup of coffee?" So she went out and bought an expensive dress—twenty-eight dollars was expensive for a young teacher on her budget—only to discover that I wore the same suit when

I picked her up. It was the only one I had at the time. We liked one another immediately.

Lesley is a great person, a very caring person. She says that we owe the success of our marriage to the personal freedom we give one another to pursue our own interests. We love to travel together; we enjoy our quiet time at home, gardening and reading; and we work together on church and community activities. Still, we don't believe we have to be together at all times. We give space to one another to be ourselves. Lesley wasn't as interested in politics as me, although she supported my interest, so I would often go to these functions on my own. One thing that made me feel good was that when I came home, no matter what time it was, I could tell her all about what happened during the evening. I could describe it with enthusiasm, and she would enjoy that. She has a very different perspective from me on many issues, and we have always enjoyed lively discussions. She has introduced me to life in England, where we travel every summer to visit with her family, and we respect and celebrate the cultural differences in our families. She is a great sounding board, and she gives me excellent advice.

We married in 1973. Soon we began to talk about starting a family. When we learned that she could not have children, we decided to adopt a baby. Then we ran into a hard brick wall of an Alberta government policy. I was over the age of forty, and at the time adoptive parents of infants had to be younger. The officials refused our request. Stupid rules. We talked about our disappointment with people, and Bruce Hogle heard about it. He was a local television broadcaster with CFRN who wrote a commentary every day. He came to our house to talk about the story, and said: "This is ridiculous." He did a news report on our situation, and I remember his commentary began: "Is Herb Belcourt too old to adopt? Was Charlie Chaplin too old to be a father?" Our case received a lot of publicity; a story also appeared in *Alberta Report*.

Helen Hunley was the social services minister in the Lougheed cabinet at the time. After all the publicity, she sent a letter to my office with a red sticker on it. She told me in the letter that the case was closed, and she would not discuss it with me again. I jumped into my car and drove straight to the legislature building. I walked into her office, past her executive assistant, Nancy MacBeth, who later became a Conservative education and health minister, and later the Alberta Liberal leader, and I walked straight past some other staff members. "Oh, you can't do that," they said, and they came after me. They were going to call security, but Helen Hunley finally said: "That's okay." She closed the door behind us.

I was exasperated with her. We wanted that baby.

We had a long, heated discussion. Finally, she promised to see if she could do something. I could have set my clock on that promise. At precisely ten o'clock on the day I returned from a holiday, the phone rang in my office. The decision had been reversed, but they threw a curve at us. We had asked to adopt a baby girl. They told us we could adopt a young girl, although not an infant, if we agreed to take her older brother.

Excited and thrilled, but nervous, we went to Calgary to meet these two children. Jolene was four and Colin was almost six. We were told about their Blackfoot tribal ancestry—their mother had been a member of the Bloods in southern Alberta—but the adoption workers told us little about their family environment, their mother's pregnancies, or their experiences as young children. That is how the adoption system worked in the 1970s. Adoptive parents had to raise children without the essential information that would be considered helpful and necessary today.

We could tell very quickly that Jolene and Colin had endured a rough start in life. When we first took them home, I think it was hell. Really hell. They would constantly take food out of the refrigerator, and we would find it hidden under their beds. We tried to teach them that they would never go hungry with us, that they would always have food while they were here. When Colin first arrived, I sat him down with me and talked about how this was his home now, that the things in it were his, too.

"Is the toaster mine, too?" he asked.

"Yes," I said.

"Well, can I have a piece of toast?"

We sat and ate toast together, but he took the idea of ownership too far. He and his sister would take things without permission. Colin would take Lesley's jewellery to school and give it away to the children as if he were buying friends. We learned they had been in ten foster homes before they came to us, and that they were in their final foster home for eighteen months or so. They were very confused little kids.

At the time we knew nothing about Fetal Alcohol Spectrum Disorder. Few people did in the 1970s. We now recognize, through our experience with the grandchildren, that Jolene and Colin both had FASD, and they both probably had Reactive Attachment Disorder (RAD), too. They had trouble forming any kind of attachment with us. A good friend, who was a family counsellor, suggested we hold Colin on our laps to try and give him a sense of belonging. We had no idea of the extent of the fetal alcohol and attachment problems. The children were diagnosed with ADHD and depression, which they had both inherited, but the other problems were not identified. We found out later that their birth father had bipolar disorder. Everything we did to try and raise them to be good citizens was totally useless, and that wasn't their fault. They needed to be raised in a different way—but we didn't know it.

We had very little concrete information. There was no disclosure in those days. Social Services had tried to have them adopted twice before, but both times the adoptions had fallen through. They wouldn't tell us any details, just that the people were willing to take one, but not both. Colin had a problem with stealing. His teacher was so amazed at his response. "I watched him go through my purse and take something," she said. When she confronted him, he cried and said, "It wasn't me." She said he was so believable, she had to stop and think, "Did I actually see this kid go in my purse?"

We had no resource people. We took the children to a private psychiatrist and he put them on a drug which we later found out they should not have been on—Nardil. They gained excessive weight. They became brilliant at school, no doubt about it, but they couldn't stop eating. Their sleep patterns changed. They woke up during the night, ready to play. They both were taking music lessons at the time. Colin was learning to play the cello and Jolene the violin. We would wake up to hear musical instruments in the night. "We are just doing our music practice," they would say. They would be ready for school at 2 AM, then they would fall asleep at school. We decided to take them off that particular drug. We later learned that Nardil is a drug that should only be used for children in their situation if Ritalin and all else fails.

Our daughter Jolene also had dysgraphia. She had an extremely high IQ, but she couldn't function at school. She could not accurately record what she knew. She even spelled her own name incorrectly. When she wrote something, it looked like scribble, but if she read it out loud to you, her ideas were absolutely amazing. The teachers at school would not hear that. They only saw the scribble, and they would say, "Do it again." Jolene lost heart. Now we have grandchildren in a school environment where the teachers understand their needs. They offer real assistance. They will say to our grandson Azlan, "Tell us what you know." He will speak and someone else will write it down for him. The difference in the outcome is positive, and remarkable.

As parents, we were ignorant of our children's needs. We loved them, but we didn't have the knowledge or understanding to help them. The school was always complaining to us: "The kids are doing this. The kids are doing that." So when Colin and Jolene came home from school, we would immediately respond to the situation: "Why are you doing this? Why are you doing that?" They were bombarded from all sides. Jolene had one teacher in Grade Two who recognized her ability, an encouraging teacher with insight, but that experience was too rare.

We tried to do the right thing for those two children. We sent them to special schools in the city where we thought they might do better. Lesley would drive an hour in the morning and an hour in the afternoon, to take them back and forth from these schools. She would drive them to music lessons and special events. We were trying to enrich their lives, take them to live theatre, give them a world to hold in their hands. Their difficulties were not their fault. They had been born with serious problems, and we did not know how to help them.

The years passed, and our troubles multiplied. Life became so bad for Colin, and for us, that we could not stand it anymore. We went to the psychiatrist Dr. Maurice Blackman at University of Alberta Hospital. "You cannot take any more of this," he told me. "You need a break. I am putting Colin in the psychiatric ward for young people with behavioural problems."

People would look at Colin and say: "What a charming, well-mannered boy." He would open doors for older people, and be a perfect gentleman. Dr. Blackman recognized that Colin had learned what face he should show to adults in order to be accepted, but when he was away from view, he would be a very different person. We put him in a temporary foster home for a little while, until he was about sixteen.

When the children came to us, they had brought family photos. All the names on the backs of the photos had been blacked out, except one. So we knew their family name. As they grew up, we asked them if they wanted to contact their birth family, to be in touch with them. They rejected the idea at first, but Colin changed his mind when he became older. He phoned the Blood reserve, where his mother had lived, and immediately learned that his birth mother had just died of an alcohol and drug overdose in Vancouver.

We all went to the funeral so Colin and Jolene could meet their biological family. Colin met his father and decided he wanted to stay with him, but Jolene decided she wanted to stay with us. She had bonded much better with us, but at the same time she had developed a very strong relationship with Colin. When he left our home, she became really upset that he was no longer around. A year later, she decided to try to go back to her family. She went to Calgary to stay with her biological grandfather, her mother's father, but none of these visits lasted long. Each visit would last a few months. From then on, Jolene and Colin drifted, backwards and forwards, to different members of their birth family. They would come home to be with us, and then they would go south again to their relatives. They were older teenagers by this time.

They were drinking. Their natural father was an alcoholic, and they fell right into it. We had not realized, of course, that they were alcoholics as babies. We also had a very limited knowledge about alcoholism. We thought they needed to learn about social drinking in moderation. We did not understand that an alcoholic can't drink at all. The addictions experts had been researching the impact of FASD at that time, but the public knew little about their findings. I had not realized that an alcoholic's brain processes alcohol differently. Instead of the alcohol turning to water, as it does in a normal brain, it turns into an opiate-like substance that accumulates in the brain.

Not long after that, Jolene became pregnant. The FASD problem was about to be passed on to a new generation in our family.

For years, we tried to help her get addiction treatment in Edmonton. We took part in the treatment programs as her parents, and we attended Al-Anon meetings in the evenings, too. I was shocked with what I learned. I had been so naïve about what alcohol does to the brain, and to the unborn child. Apparently, as early as 1899, studies in England linked alcohol consumption during pregnancy to poor birth outcomes for women in prisons. Researchers in France in 1968 noted birth defects in children born to alcoholic mothers. So it has taken us a long time to get this far, and it has been a struggle.

Around this time I began to work with other Albertans to convince the provincial government, particularly the people responsible for children's services, that FASD was an illness. I took part in a team that put guidelines together before the new policies went to cabinet for approval. I remember going to a Conservative convention in Calgary where the issue came up. We broke up into small discussion groups to ask questions of the cabinet ministers, and when the FASD question was raised, one lady said: "This is not our problem." I saw red and I jumped up to say so. I have to thank Drew Hutton, and some other Conservative members, including a doctor, who came to my defence, because they knew how furious I was about this attitude. Alberta now recognizes FASD as an illness and is working hard on prevention policies.

Our jails are full of prisoners with FASD. What a terrible cost to society this syndrome has become. Sometimes I think the jails would be empty if we could get rid of this problem. Think of the medical and educational costs we could avoid, but even more important, think of the human suffering we could spare our children if we worked harder to prevent the addiction problems of pregnant mothers.

We tried to help Colin go to AA meetings, but he had a very difficult time with alcohol addiction, too. He used to phone us, but he was usually drunk. He asked us for money to start a business, which we gave him, and we also built a house for him, but these things fell through. Eventually, we said, "That's it. We have done our bit. That's it." Sadly, we have no contact with him. He doesn't phone. It is a shame that he has so much difficulty with addictions, because he was actually a hard worker. He worked as a dishwasher at our restaurant. Later he became a cook and then he started painting houses. He worked hard, earned good money, but it was all lost on drink. He probably could have had a successful business if alcohol had not been such a problem.

Many people with FASD have poor adaptive skills and do not see the consequences of their actions. They may have difficulty regulating their behaviour, and often have mood swings. They may act impulsively and make poor choices and decisions.

Jolene was more willing to try to get help. She had given birth to a baby boy when she was seventeen, but the infant died a few hours later. Sometimes she would come north to live with us. We would welcome her back home, set her up in a place, or help her to return to resume her education, all at her request. Everything would be set up. Then we would get up in the morning and find her bedroom empty and a note on the bed: "Sorry, I can't do it." She would go away again. We would not even know where she was. So we said: "Let's do this in a civilized way. No more climbing out of windows. You go, and do whatever you want, but keep in touch."

When my granddaughter Amethyst was born, I was right there in the room. It was the first time I had ever seen a human being born, and I will cherish the memory forever. It was like a miracle. The little body fit right into my hand. At home, the baby would lie in bed between Lesley and me, and she would always hold my little finger and kiss my nose. I remember the joy of watching Lesley and Amethyst playing on the floor when she was only a few months old. Every now and then, I look back at these pictures in my mind. I would take Amethyst into the garden when she was a baby, and point out the flowers. She would look at the flowers with interest, as if she understood every word I said.

Jolene stayed in our home with Amethyst until the baby was six months old. She had already separated from her boyfriend, because there was a lot of abuse going on there, and he ended up in jail. She made one good choice, and said: "I'm not going to wait for him, but I want to go back to the reserve." She was twenty-one. Her troubles were not over. There was an occasion when we took the baby from her apartment because we were concerned about her well-being. Jolene called the police to get the baby back. The RCMP tried to reason with her and said, "Look, right now, this is a better place for the baby to be." However, they told us they couldn't make her leave the baby with us. In the past, we had tended to be dogmatic, and tell Jolene what to do, but we knew we needed to preserve the relationship. It was her choice. She left with the baby, but every so often, she would phone us and ask whether we would like to have Amethyst for a visit. We knew that another drinking session was a possibility, so we would welcome her to bring the baby. Amethyst would sometimes stay with us for six months at a time.

Azlan was born in 1997, when Amethyst was one and a half. He was premature. Azlan's father was still living with Jolene at the time, and we think he was the one taking caring of the little boy much of the time. The couple separated a few years later. We were visiting Disneyland with Amethyst—she was about four at this point—when we received a phone call from Social Services in British Columbia.

"Have you still got Amethyst?" the social worker said. "Have you sent her back to her mother yet?"

"No, we haven't," I said.

"Please, don't send her back. We have had to apprehend Azlan and he is now in a foster home."

We asked if we could take him, and we put that plan in motion. Lesley flew to BC to pick him up, and we brought him home. A friend of ours, a lawyer, recommended that we ask the court for legal custody of both children. Jolene and Azlan's father agreed that this was the best idea, so they signed the documents. We went to court. Lesley had written some background for the court about the children's lives, about six pages, but the judge said: "I don't need to read past the first page. You have custody. You have legal guardianship and custody."

We didn't adopt the children. We recognize that Amethyst and Azlan are Jolene's children. They are our grandchildren. We also know that both of them were born with FASD and related problems. Amethyst had a very difficult time as a young child after contacts with her mother. We didn't want to stop the visits or phone calls with Jolene, because we thought they were a good thing. The psychiatrist has recommended that the children have no contact with her until she can be sober for at least one year. So that's what we did. It has been very tough.

Jolene was in southern Alberta the last time we heard. She had made a very positive step forward, going back to school to follow her childhood dream of becoming a veterinarian's assistant. Pressured by her boyfriend, she dropped out. She returned to school and was voted class president, but she dropped out again. She is a very likeable, intelligent person with wonderful speaking skills; she has won prizes for public speaking. She is a beautiful human being. We pray that she will eventually make use of her talents and reach her potential.

Our experience with FASD is completely different now that we are raising our grandchildren in a more progressive time. The syndrome is better understood now: by us, by the medical profession, and by teachers in the public education system. Specialists can diagnose children early. We were able to get Amethyst and Azlan into a pilot program for FASD through Dr. Gail Andrew at the Glenrose Rehabilitation Hospital in Edmonton. That diagnosis opened the door for all of us. Dr. Andrew was a member of a team that developed clinical practice guidelines for the prevention and diagnosis of FASD. She also helped to establish the clinic at Glenrose to diagnose FASD, and to provide support to families. For us, the diagnosis meant our grandchildren had special help in education. It meant we had access to community support and respite care when we needed it, through the Robin Hood Association in Sherwood Park. This excellent community organization has provided services and programs to people with disabilities and to their families since 1963. We have benefited greatly from the Robin Hood's family support services.

We are grateful for this help. The early intervention has been wonderful for our grandchildren, and for us. We have access to the correct medications. We have had the assistance of a wonderful psychiatrist, and the excellent staff members at the Glenrose Hospital School in Edmonton. The school's behavioural program helps children cope with the consequences of FASD.

Our own attitude is different this time. With our children, we had been advised to be very strict, when in fact they really needed a much more gentle, loving environment with strong guidelines. Our children were hampered at school, and at home, when we reminded them repeatedly that they were not working, not trying. In contrast, our grandchildren attend a wonderful local school where they are supported and encouraged every step of the way. I am most grateful to the staff at Pine Street School here in Sherwood Park for going that extra step, and helping raise the self-esteem of both children by believing in them. Today Alberta Learning has even produced a book titled *Teaching Children with FASD*. How education changes!

Now we understand that our grandchildren have difficulties. We have adjusted our expectations. We understand that if their experiences are difficult, there is a reason, and we can help them. We are there to support them, to encourage them, to remind them that every step forward they make is a good one—just as their teachers are doing at school. It is wonderful. We have been given a second chance. We intend to do it right this time.

Amethyst is a lovely girl. She is as smart as a whip, very quick on her feet, and she would make a wonderful speaker if we could just encourage that. She has a beautiful singing voice, but she doesn't want to take lessons. We hear her singing in her room, and she picks up music on the piano; with one finger she will pick out the notes. She enjoys that, and it's lovely. I can be sitting quietly in the den, and all of a sudden I hear her at the piano. Beautiful.

Azlan is a caring little boy. He is coming along really well. He has a heart of gold, and he loves nature. He enjoys watching nature programs on television, and he can tell you all about the fish in the ocean, the birds, the wildlife in the forest, what they eat, how many teeth they have. He is brilliant, I think. Sometimes he has trouble expressing himself, but he teaches me a lot in his own way. Once I took him golfing at Waterton Lakes National Park, when he was only four, and he said: "Grandpa, I don't think I like that game." I asked him what he would prefer to do. "I want to watch the birds and butterflies," he said. He pointed to a hummingbird at a feeder nearby, and told me what it was. I enjoyed playing with him that day. That is a memory I treasure.

It isn't easy to talk about the most painful experiences in family life. Lesley and I have decided to speak openly about the FASD problem in our family with the hope that we can take the sting out of it for other Canadians. We understand that some people are reluctant to talk about serious addiction problems in their families. They feel too ashamed, too sad, or too weary to discuss the terrible damage that alcohol and drugs might have imposed on a loved child during a pregnancy. We don't blame anyone for these uneasy feelings. It is not so many years ago that

We are raising our grandchildren, Amethyst and Azlan.

doctors were actually advising pregnant women to relax with a glass of wine. How confusing is that?

We believe that Canadians, all of us together, need to speak openly about FASD in our families. We should tell children and teenagers in the schools about what alcohol and drugs can do to an unborn child. We have to be wide open about it, because it is obvious that many young parents don't know the serious, lifelong consequences of drinking or drug abuse during pregnancy. We need to take one step at a time until we can reduce or get rid of this problem, and we won't succeed until we get the story out into the open. Lesley and I are trying to do what we can. We encourage other families to move forward to improve the situation.

We hope we can raise our own grandchildren to create a better environment for themselves. I hope they won't touch alcohol or drugs. They have seen how it has affected their own lives, so I hope they will make good choices and reach their full potential. We hope we have been a good example to them.

If we can teach all children that illegal drugs and alcohol are harmful, especially once a woman conceives, this would be a better world. That's what I want to teach our two grandchildren. They don't have to have a drink to have a good time. They can go out for dinner, they can go anywhere, and enjoy a non-alcoholic drink. We have taught them that. We have told them that some children are diabetic and can't eat too much sugar, and some children have serious allergies and can't eat peanuts or peanut butter. We are teaching them that they can't touch alcohol and drugs for similar reasons.

Parents and grandparents have ten or twelve years—a time when a window is open and not shut—when we can reach our children, and teach them how to end the FASD cycle forever. We can't do it alone. We have to do it together.

CHAPTER FOURTEEN

Two Sons

K IM AND DAVID, MY TWO older sons from my first marriage, grew up to follow very different paths in life. Kim, the younger one, was the happy-go-lucky child, always in a circle of friends; David, the older one, was the calm little boy who liked to read and enjoyed gardening.

As an adult, Kim ran Lord Belcourt Formal Wear for a time, and was interested in business. He eventually left to begin an independent life of his own in northern Alberta. David worked hard with Belcourt Construction for many years. They both have blessed me with grandchildren.

One day in 1978, when he was only twenty-eight years old, David returned from a work road trip and said: "Dad, I don't know what's the matter, but I don't know if I can go into the mountain area anymore. My feet are just burning." I advised him to see a doctor. He returned to me after the appointment, looking devastated. "The doctor suspects multiple sclerosis," he said.

With Kim and David, my sons from my first marriage.

We had our hugs. I advised him to seek a second opinion. The doctors did a spinal tap and confirmed that he had MS, a very challenging type in which all the nerve endings are raw. David suffered great pain at times. Several years later, I could not even put my arm around him, or over his shoulders, without adding to the pain. The MS would go into remission at times, but it would return. He could be blind for a time, and then his hearing would go and he would be deaf.

He stayed on the job as long as he could, but he was soon unable to work. He was able to live in his own home for a long time, with help, and he kept a beautiful garden. At that time, I used to take him hot meals from our restaurant. David is fifty-two now, and he lives in Dickensfield Long Term Care Centre. He has lost his short-term memory, but he still manages to enjoy his life. He has a wonderful friend named Susan Hunting. She has looked after him, taking him out on outings on the North Saskatchewan River and around the city. She goes to his house in Mill Woods every day to feed his cats, and she takes him to his home, which he still owns, when he is able to go. I try to talk to him every week, and I visit him every two weeks. David's son Matthew is a fine young man who is working in British Columbia, playing percussion with a small band.

Kim attended the Northern Alberta Institute of Technology and became a qualified insulator. He was at the top of his graduating class. I remember how proud he was. He married when he was very young, and he and his wife had a son, David Herb, a delightful young man who always has a smile on his face. He works very hard as a painter in British Columbia. Kim's first wife died. His daughter, Jenna, is from his second marriage. Jenna's mother has raised a wonderful girl. It is a pleasure for me whenever I see her. I see Kim occasionally. We golf together from time to time.

Can I say this? I love my children and grandchildren very much.

CHAPTER FIFTEEN

Gordon's Search

I BEGAN THIS STORY LOOKING FOR my grandfather's land, and a trail I used to know, near Lac
Ste. Anne. I have become more interested in the history
of the area because it is one of Alberta's oldest Métis
communities. I realize how much more I have to learn
about our family roots. Some parts of the story remain
a mystery to me.

I invited my brother Gordon to my house to talk
about the history of our family. He is the historian in
the Belcourt clan. He has spent thirty years searching
for documents about the Métis of the Lac Ste. Anne
area—about our great-grandfather Magloire Belcourt,
his land, and what happened to that land.

Gordon also discovered that our extended family is
related through marriage to members of the Papaschase
and Enoch Cree bands of the Edmonton area. Over the
generations, Métis families of Lac Ste. Anne have also
intermarried with members of the nearby Alexander,

Alexis, and Michel bands. All five First Nations claimed reserves in the Edmonton area when their chiefs and headmen signed adhesions to Treaty 6 at Fort Edmonton on August 21, 1877, and on September 18, 1878. About a decade later, after the Northwest Rebellion, the government of Canada sent scrip commissioners to this part of western Canada. Their job was to "satisfy any claims existing in connection with the extinguishment of Indian title." They offered scrip coupons to people of mixed ancestry, including people who had already been identified as Indians under Treaty 6. Scrip coupons could be exchanged for 240 acres of Crown land, but many people sold them to scrip speculators or middlemen for less than the face value. The commissioners took one thousand scrip applications in Edmonton in June 1885, and hundreds more the next summer in Edmonton and St. Albert. In the crowds, somewhere, were my ancestors.

The Papaschase people lost their reserve in what is now south Edmonton in 1889. Some of the remaining band members were transferred to the Enoch band, and they moved to that reserve, and others moved away across western Canada. The Papaschase descendants are still disputing the loss of their land in legal challenges to the federal government.

Through his years of research, Gordon has assembled many documents that Native people in Edmonton have been looking for. I would like to see these documents available to all Cree, Métis, and Nakoda people—and to the public so that Albertans will have a richer understanding of the true history of this part of Canada.

We are also very fortunate to own a copy of a

documented family tree that traces the Belcourt and the Callihoo families back to 1750.

This genealogy exists thanks to a little American baby born in Redwood City, California, in 1954. The child's mother had a rare genetic condition—called Rare D Chromosome Deletion—that can result in incompatibility between a mother and her unborn baby, causing a miscarriage. The Californian needed a blood transfusion to deliver her infant by C-section, but public health authorities knew of only four matches in the world. An emergency call went out to the international Red Cross for another match. By coincidence, a Mrs. L'Hirondelle of Lac Ste. Anne, married to J. Alex L'Hirondelle, needed a blood transfusion at the Misericordia Hospital after a sixth miscarriage. Doctors discovered she had the same rare gene. Her sister, Jean, was a match. A number of family members quickly donated blood to save the California baby, and build up the supply for other people in need. Public health authorities went by truck to the Michel reserve, west of St. Albert, and rushed the shipment to Edmonton; a Canadian air force plane made the emergency flight to California.

Public health authorities in Edmonton also decided to test other family members. Dr. D.I. Buchanan, the provincial medical director, and Dr. P.E. Moore, the director of Indian Health Services, asked two dedicated people to conduct genealogical research to identify possible donors. Miss Gilda Graves, later Gilda Roth, was a nurse employed by the Department of Indian Affairs at the Camsell Hospital. Emile Tardif was an Oblate priest and historian. Working together for two months, they conducted intensive research—through birth, baptism, marriage, and death certificates, government documents, and personal interviews—to trace the intertwined families of the old voyageurs Joseph Belcourt and Louis Callihoo. They traced more than 1,650 people through six generations back to 1750. They collected 150 blood specimens and found twenty-four people with the rare blood condition. Their final research findings were presented at an international conference of blood specialists in Paris, France, in 1954; a Canadian geneticist, Dr. Bruce Cowan, described the research as "the richest thing in genetics that has been discovered in a long time."

It was even richer for us. Looking carefully at these genealogical charts, and comparing the names and birthdates to other historical documents, Gordon has been able to determine, for example, that our maternal ancestors Catherine L'Hirondelle, Nancy Belcourt, and Cecile Belcourt had treaty status at one time. The Métis, Cree, Nakoda, and Cree-Iroquois families of the historic Beaver Hills area, along the North Saskatchewan River, up to St. Albert and Lac Ste. Anne and Wabamun, north past Morinville to Alexander, and all around the old Fort Edmonton—the people of *amiskwaciwâskahikan*—were often close relatives. That remains true today. We have a shared territory, and a shared history.

Gordon has more to say about his research and what he has discovered. It is his turn to speak.

GORDON BELCOURT

I was born on June 22, 1938, and I grew up near Lac Ste. Anne. I was always interested in history in school. For me, it was a subject I thrived on. I just found it very interesting as I grew up. I married Lola Sinclair, who has Métis family roots that go way back through many generations into the Métis of the Red River settlement. One of her ancestors was a chief factor for the Hudson's Bay Company. In 1841, another Métis trader named James Sinclair led an expedition of twenty-three Métis families—121 people in all—from Manitoba across the Prairies and over the Rockies to settle in the Oregon territory at the request of the Hudson's Bay Company. Another member of her family, Benjamin Sinclair, came west from Norway House with his wife, Margaret Collins, to work with Reverend Robert Rundle at the Methodist mission at Pigeon Lake, south of Fort Edmonton, in 1847. Benjamin worked at missions at Pigeon Lake, Lac La Biche, and Whitefish Lake before he died in 1884. He is buried in the same grave as Henry Bird Steinhauer, another Native missionary.

My wife and I wanted to know more about where we came from and who we were. Were we treaty people or Métis people, or possibly both?

I started out by looking for historical documents about Lac Ste. Anne, but many were in French, which I couldn't understand. I was involved with the Native Council of Canada in the 1970s and 1980s, and on my own time, I began to research documents at the National Archives of Canada in Ottawa. I had a friend there, who helped me. I must have made thirty or forty visits. It cost me a fortune. I came home with files full of copied documents about the agreements between the federal government and the Papaschase and Enoch bands near Edmonton, the breakup of the Papaschase reserve, and the transfer of the so-called "Edmonton Stragglers" to the Enoch band.

I began to get more interested in learning about Louis Karakonti, also known as Louis Callihoo, who came west with my ancestor Joseph Belcourt through the Athabasca waterways. There are twenty-one ways in which the Church changed Louis' last name. He has descendants at Noah's Creek, south of Grande Prairie, and out at Grande Cache. Louis Callihoo's daughter married Joseph Belcourt's son, and that couple had Magloire Belcourt, our great-grandfather.

One of Louis Callihoo's sons, Michel Callihoo, signed an adhesion to Treaty 6 in 1878 and claimed a reserve for his large family and other related members of our community under treaty. These people became known as treaty Indians in the Michel band. The Michel reserve, located west of St. Albert, existed between the 1880s and March 31, 1958, when the government of Canada enfranchised the band, at the request of a majority of members on the reserve. (Later, about five hundred descendants of the Michel band regained their treaty status through Bill C-31, and they applied to the government of Canada for formal recognition and a land base. Today, some of these descendants are still working to achieve their goal.)

I learned that some women in the Belcourt family had at one time belonged to the Papaschase and, later, Enoch bands, and were recognized under treaty. Everything we found pointed to the fact that we were related to people with treaty status, as far as I was concerned. Yet we were denied that status because some ancestors took Métis scrip, on both sides of the family. We learned that other families that took Métis scrip at the same time eventually got their treaty status back.

Whenever we inquired about possible treaty rights,

we were told that our great-grandparents took scrip. Scrip, as I understand it, came about around the time the government of Canada hanged Louis Riel. The people in Ottawa wanted to quiet down the trouble that was in the country, so they gave scrip.

It seems to me that that there are Métis people who should have treaty status, and status Indians who are, in fact, Métis people. On many reserves, the documentation proves that beyond question. If you look at the history, the Papaschase and Enoch reserves were set up as agreements between the government of the first prime minister, Sir John A. Macdonald, and the two bands. It is a contract signed between Canada and a group of people, including members of my family. There are Belcourt descendants with treaty status at Enoch and at Hobbema.

I was trying to find out where I came from, and what was important about it, but I always asked the same question: What is so important about bloodlines? I never got an answer, and nobody can give it to me.

I gave copies of the family tree to my two sons and two daughters. I told everyone they were welcome to it. "At least you will know who you are," I said, "whether you are status or not." It makes no difference to me. I could never understand why bloodlines and nationality meant so much to some people. Everybody is a human being in this world, but people say, "I am English . . . I am Ukrainian . . . I am Indian . . . I am Chinese . . . I am Jewish." Our blood is the same colour, isn't it? We all live more or less the same way. Our women are made the same, our men are made the same, so why is there such conflict? That is what I could never understand. Once I asked a cabinet minister in Ottawa to consider a possibility. "You talk about your French bloodlines. You tell me your family has had five generations in Canada. If I followed your family, I would prove you have Native blood in you. If you have five generations in this country, you have Native blood, too." He wouldn't believe me. "Why do you make the bloodline so important?" I asked. "If you had to take my blood as a transfusion to survive, would you be French or would you be Métis?" He just turned beet red after that.

After the research I did, I have learned the truth about what happened in our country. I am ashamed of some of it. It was disappointing. There was discrimination against so many people: the farmers in the Hungry Thirties who were going to Ottawa to demonstrate, the Hutterites, the Ukrainians, the Doukhobor children who were taken away from their families in the 1950s—and the Native people, of course, all the way through. Canadians like to talk about human rights abuses around the world. We had better look at our own closet, full of skeletons. If people in Canada knew all the history, I don't think they would believe everything that has happened in this country.

I found one injustice related to our family when I was doing my research. I found the will of my great-grand-father, Magloire Belcourt, who died at Lac Ste. Anne on August 8, 1908. The probate order says that he had household belongings worth fifty dollars, two wagons and harnesses worth one hundred dollars, horses worth three hundred dollars, cattle worth eighty dollars, and his family's land. In his will he left all of his property to his widow and his eight children. His will says he owned a quarter-section with mineral rights to Lots 22 and 23 in Lac Ste. Anne, and all of River Lot 9, except two acres.

The probate order describes the legal description of the land as Lot 9 in Lac Ste. Anne settlement, except two acres, valued at nine hundred dollars, and a quarter-section [18-54-3W-5] valued at eight hundred dollars. The executors of his estate were Peter Gunn and Leger Lambert.

Our family had some of the land at Lac Ste. Anne until my father sold it, but I believe the Catholic Church ended up with some of the land in Magloire's will. I put a legal caveat on it, meaning that the Church would not be allowed to sell it until it had dealt with my objection. The former Archbishop Joseph McNeil contacted me. I sat in his office on 116th Street and Jasper Avenue, meeting with him, and what he said to me I won't repeat. He definitely was against the caveat. He even accused me of not being a good Catholic, and I said, "Well, you are a lot poorer Catholic than me if you are defending what was done." I said, "I am only asking for what belongs to the family. It doesn't belong to you or the Church." I walked out of his office after three or four meetings, and I wouldn't go back. I never heard anything about the caveat. The land in question was sold.

I am proud that my great-grandparents were explorers and voyageurs. They helped to develop this country, and no one gave them a cent of the credit. The most important thing to remember about all of our great-grandparents, right down the line, is that they were independent. We still are.

I haven't really found out who I am yet. Everything points in a different direction, and I don't know which to believe. The people should know what happened. At least our great-grandchildren will be able to read this book, and know it.

What follows are selected documents related to Métis and Cree land in Edmonton and Lac Ste. Anne, from Gordon Belcourt's collection.

Treaty No.6.

North-West Territories.

INDIAN RESERVE NO.136.

Area 39.9 square miles,

Number of families in Band - 38,

Name of Chief - "Papaschase" alias "The Woodpecker"

Surveyed in September 1884, by J.C.Nelson D.L.S.

(The survey was commenced in 1880 by G.A.Simpson,DLS

This reserve is situated at the Two Hills, five miles south of Edmonton on the Calgary trail.

It is bounded by a line beginning at a post in mound, twenty-eight chains and forty-six links, more or less, north, and seventy-one chains and seventy-five links, more or less, west, of the north-east corner of Section seven, Township fifty-two, Range twenty-four, West of the Fourth Initial Meridian; thence running east five hundred and sixty chains, more or less, to a post; thence south four hundred and fifty-three chains and forty-three links, more or less, to a post; thence west five hundred and sixty-two chains and seven links, more or less, to a post; and thence north four hundred and fifty-seven chains and fourteen links to the point of beginning; containing an area of thirty-nine and nine-tenths square miles, more or less.

White-mud Creek flows in a northerly direction through the south-western end of the reserve; the lands best adapted for cultivation lie along this stream. The eastern part is much

broken

12

broken by swamps and ponds in which the water varies with the dryness of the season. There are numerous swamps and prairie openings, affording pea vine and vetches of great luxuriance. The soil is a rich black loam. A greater portion of the surface is thickly covered with scrub and poplar. Some spruce, birch and tamarac are found along the western and southern boundaries. Ruffed grouse abound in the thickets along the latter.

This is the first page of a Treaty 6 adhesion document describing the Papaschase Cree reserve in the land that is now south Edmonton. The chief Papastayo, or Papaschase, brought his band into treaty in 1877, and the reserve was surveyed in 1880. Under pressure from white settlers in Edmonton, the Papaschase band lost its reserve of almost forty square miles in 1888.

8

IN WITNESS WHEREOF, we have hereunto set our hands and affixed our seals this *Nineteenth* day of *November* in the year of Our Lord one thousand eight hundred and *Eighty eight*

Signed. Sealed and Delivered,
in the presence of

*having been first interpreted and
explained to said Napason,
James Stony and Antoine*

(sgd) John Calder
Interpreter
Stony Plain

(sgd) Joseph O'Keldchl
Advocate
Edmonton

(sgd) John Calder

(sgd) *Napason* his X mark (L.S.)

" *James Stony* his X mark (L.S.)

" *Antoine* his X mark (L.S.)

(L.S.)

(L.S.)

This is the final page of the "surrender document," which released the Papaschase reserve to the federal government and opened up the land to white settlement. Neither the chief nor his brothers signed the document; it carries the names of only three band members. Note that the three X-marks are identical.

No. 404   Form J.

DEPARTMENT OF THE INTERIOR, CANADA,

NORTH WEST HALF-BREED COMMISSION.

St Albert 9° June 1885

This is to Certify that *Maglorie Belcourt*
a Half-Breed, has proved to the satisfaction of the Commission that he was residing in the North West Territories previous to the 15th day of July, 1870, and under Sub-clause **(E)** of Clause 81 of the Dominion Lands Act, 1883, and the Order in Council of the 30th March, 1885, is entitled at this date to Scrip to the amount of *Two hundred and forty* dollars.

The Scrip called for by this Certificate, amounting to *Two hundred + forty* dollars, will be payable to bearer, will specify the name of the person in whose favour it is granted, and will be delivered to the person producing this Certificate. Said Scrip will be accepted at par in payment of Dominion Lands.

Wm R Shut

Chairman of the Commission.

The Canadian government offered scrip to the Métis of Edmonton, St. Albert, and Lac Ste. Anne in the summer of 1885, just a few months after the Northwest Rebellion and the hanging of Louis Riel. Scrip was a certificate that could be redeemed in $240 or 240 acres of homestead land. This was Ottawa's response to the land grievances of the Métis at a time when white settlers were moving into their traditional territory. My great-grandfather, Magloire Belcourt, applied for scrip in St. Albert in June 1885, and he received this certificate.

A commissioner's note recording payment of $240 in scrip to my great-grandfather in 1885.

Declaration by _Magloire Belcourt_

Concerning _his_ **Claim**

to participate in any grant to Half-Breeds living in the

North-West Territories. _as a halfbreed chil_

1. What is your name and P. O. Address? _St Albert P.O. (Residence Lac Ste anne)_

2. Where and when were you born? _May 1855 Lac Ste anne_

3. What was the name of your father? _Baptiste Belcourt_

4. What was the name of your mother? _Cecile Calia_

5. Was your father a Half-breed or Indian or either? _Halfbreed_

6. Was your mother a Half-breed or Indian or either? _do_

7. Where were you living each year since you were born? _I have always lived at Lac Ste anne with my parents up to the date of my marriage_

8. What has been your occupation? _Farmer & labourer_

9. If married when, where and to whom? _In 1879 Constance Original at Lac Ste anne_

10. How many children have you living? _Three_

11. Give their names, and dates of birth? _Jean Bte, 4 apprais 4 age, Pierre 2½, Virn 1½_

12. What was the name of their respective (mothers or fathers as the case may be)

13. How many children had you who died? _None_

14. Give dates of birth and death of those who died?

My great-grandfather's application for scrip. These applications have become rich sources of information about Métis family history, as they record birthplaces, family lineage, and occupations in early western Canada.

I, _Magloire Belcourt_ within named, make oath (or declare) and say that the within answers given by me are true in every particular. So help me God.

Sworn (or declared) before me, at _St. Albert_ this _9th_ day of _9 June_ A.D., 188 _5_ — having been first read over and explained in the _French_ language to the deponent, who seemed perfectly to understand the same, and in my presence. _made her mark thereto_

his
Magloire X Belcourt
mark

W.P. N. Hunt *Junior*

Commissioner

We _Adolphe Perrain & Augustin Claudie of St. Alb_ make oath (or declare) and say that *we* know _Magloire Belcourt_, who has made oath to the correctness of the within answers, and so far as his answers to questions numbered _3, 4, 5, 6 & 7_ are concerned, I know them to be correct, and so far as the remainder are concerned, *we* believe them to be true and correct in every particular.

Sworn (or declared) before me, at _St Albert_ this _9th_ day of _June_ A.D., 188 _5_ — having been first read over and explained in the _French_ language to the deponent, who seemed perfectly to understand the same, and in my presence. _the said Adolphe signed the same and the said Augustin made his mark thereto_

Adolphe Perrain
his
Augustin X Claudie
mark

W.P. N. Hunt

Commissioner

My great-grandfather, Magloire, signed his scrip application
with an X after hearing an explanation in French.

Gordon found this photocopy of federal cabinet notes related to "the extinguishment of the Indian title preferred by Half Breeds resident in the Northwest Territories outside of the limits of Manitoba." The signature appears to be that of Sir John A. Macdonald, Canada's first prime minister.

at one dollar per acre; the
area in no case to exceed forty
acres and payment therefor
to be made within two years

2. That in satisfaction
of their claims as actual settlers
upon these small water frontages
which are proposed to be sold to
them they be permitted to
select from lands open for
homestead and preemption
entry as nearly as possible
in the vicinity of their holdings
one quarter section of 160 acres
more or less the patent for
which however shall not issue
until payment has been made
in full for the lands of which
they are now in occupation
as

as aforesaid.

3. That in the case of
children of half-breed heads
of families residing in the
North West Territories prior
to the 15ᵗʰ day of July 1870 and
born before that date instead
of an issue of $240. in scrip
they be granted a certificate
entitling them to select 240 acres
of land from any lands open
for homestead and preemption
entry.

John A Macdonald

app'd

Lansdowne

18. 4. 05

APR 2 8 1986

Mr. Gordon J. Belcourt
R.R. No. 1, Site 15
P.O. Box 14
SPRUCE GROVE, Alberta
T0E 2C0

Dear Mr. Belcourt:

Thank you for your letter of February 21, 1986 and the documentation
in support of your claim to entitlement to Indian status.

Mr. Les Smith, the Registrar, has confirmed that
Jean Baptiste Belcourt, who has been identified as your paternal
grandfather, took scrip in 1901. Further, Elzear Laroque took scrip
in 1901 on behalf of himself and his family including Marie Rose, who
has been identified as your paternal grandmother. The Registrar has
been unable to identify Florence Courtoreille, your mother, as having
been a member of an Indian band before her marriage to your father
Alfred-Wilfrid Belcourt.

Unfortunately, therefore, as the descendant of persons who accepted
scrip, you were not entitled to registration as an Indian under
paragraph 12(1)(a)(ii) of the Indian Act as it read immediately prior
to April 17, 1985. In addition, the 1985 amendments to the
Indian Act did not include any provision permitting the registration
of persons who took scrip and their descendants. Consequently, the
Registrar has concluded that you are not eligible under the
Indian Act to be registered as an Indian.

I am taking this opportunity of returning your documents to you.
Kindest regards.

Sincerely,

David Crombie

Encls. (4)

Gordon wrote to David Crombie, a former Minister of Indian Affairs, to inquire
whether the Belcourt family could claim Indian status, as some of our ancestors
had entered Treaty 6 in the Edmonton area. He received this reply from Ottawa.

AUGUST 10, 1981

MOST REVEREND JOSEPH N. MACNEIL
ARCHBISHOP OF EDMONTON
10044 113TH STREET
EDMONTON, ALBERTA
        T5K 1N8

DEAR SIR:

AFTER SOME CONSIDERABLE THOUGHT I AM WRITING TO YOU CONCERNING AN OLD
MATTER INVOLVING LAC STE. ANNE. ATTACHED YOU WILL FIND A COPY OF THE
WILL OF MAGLOIRE BELCOURT, A LONG-TIME RESIDENT OF LAC STE. ANNE.
AS YOU SEE HE MAKES REFERENCE TO 2 ACRES OF LAND, NOW HELD IN THE
NAME OF THE ROMAN CATHOLIC CHURCH ON THE "SOUTH SIDE OF THE TRAIL"
(NOW THE HIGHWAY). AS MAGLOIRE WAS MY GREAT GRANDFATHER, I SHOULD
LIKE MY FAMILY TO HAVE WHAT IS RIGHTFULLY THEIRS.
COULD YOU HAVE YOUR SOLICITOR LOOK INTO THIS, AND CONTACT EITHER
MYSELF AT R.R. #1, SITE 15, P.O. BOX 14, SPRUCE GROVE, ALBERTA (962-4228)
OR MY COLLEAGUE RICHARD LONG AT #101-10324 119TH STREET, EDMONTON,
ALBERTA (482-6294).

                              YOURS TRULY,

GB/lb
                              GORDON BELCOURT

Gordon's note to Archbishop Joseph McNeil of Edmonton,
inquiring about a portion of Magloire Belcourt's original land.

CHAPTER SIXTEEN

Destinations

MY STORY IS ALMOST FINISHED. I will celebrate my seventy-fifth birthday in July 2006. At this time in my life, I don't want to have any more business pressures or problems of any kind. I want to enjoy my family and my friendships, the odd game of crib, and more travelling with Lesley and our grandchildren. Travel is an education for all of us. We can see how others live, and understand that there is no single way to do things. I want to continue trying to help in the community, trying to solve the drug problem, if that is ever possible. I like talking to people and assisting where I can, and then I like to come home to do a bit of gardening, because I enjoy being among the flowers.

I have a few more things to say to friends and strangers who might read this book.

I would like to speak directly to Native high school students, who continue to experience racism and discrimination and get discouraged about it.

Returning to my roots.

BE PROUD OF who you are and where you come from. Never be ashamed of your culture or family background. Every culture has something worthwhile to offer the world. Those who belittle you are not worth your time, so don't waste it on them. So many people in the past, and in my generation, did not acknowledge their Native heritage because of discrimination. Today, it is amazing how many people are identifying themselves as Native. They feel good about it, and you should too. One counselling method advises kids how to stay cool in a conflict. Don't get hot (angry), don't get cold (keeping your distance, with hostility), but quietly approach the taunting kids (stay cool) and make a statement such as: "I find your comments offensive, and I would like you to stop." Or ask a question: "What exactly do you know about Métis culture? I can recommend a good book." This approach won't silence the worst of them, but it will make you feel better. Who will get the last laugh once you get an education, and move ahead in your life? The people who put you down, or you? You will.

If you belong to a family that can't afford to help you get started in life, or help to pay your tuition, I hope you will apply for a Belcourt Brosseau Student Award. Whatever you do, don't give up. Follow your dream. There are so many scholarships out there that will help you pay for your living expenses, child care, transportation, and tuition. Education is a powerful tool for eliminating poverty. If you have the will to succeed, you will find the way. Think of how proud your parents—and your future children—will be when you reach the goals you have set for yourself. You can only be a winner. The only way to lose is to give up.

When I think about what I have achieved without an education, I always imagine what I might have done if I had had one! So many young people leave school before they have proven themselves. You have to be strong, and determined, to stay on the path. Make that promise to yourself—nobody else. If you take that step, and complete your education, you will have succeeded on your own. You will gain an enormous amount of satisfaction—and no drug can give you the high that comes with that kind of satisfaction.

When you graduate, encourage the next generation to follow you into post-secondary education so that they will set their children on the right path of self-esteem and dignity. Let them see that there *is* something worthwhile at the end of that path.

Perhaps you dream about working for yourself, starting your own business, but you have no financial resources. No bank or lender will lend you money without collateral. Have you looked into the possibility of going to relatives and friends, or perhaps to an economic development agency like the Métis-controlled Apeetogosan? You would need approximately six months of funding for staying power. Before you ask for financial assistance, make sure you have done a market study. Is this business dream feasible? What is the need? Do other companies need your service? Don't allow yourself to be negative. If you have no relatives or friends able to lend you money, and if you have decided that your idea is workable, try to cut back on your own spending and save some money to obtain collateral. Never go to a high-interest commercial money mart or money lender. Try to be stringent, and stay out of debt. The banker will see that you have saved,

"Be proud of yourself. Be proud of your Métis heritage."

that you are not in debt, and might be impressed enough to help you. If you believe in yourself, other people will believe in you. I already believe in you.

We live in a consumer society that tries to make us feel dissatisfied with ourselves. We are urged constantly to look outside ourselves for happiness. We are told to buy this and buy that, and then we will be happy. We are told to change the way we look, and then we will be happy.

The true source of happiness comes from within yourself. No person can give it to you or take it away. You don't have to impress anyone except yourself. Be proud of yourself. Be proud of your heritage. Make a promise to yourself, and keep it.

I HAVE HAD a rich life. I feel fortunate because I have been involved in a wide range of activities.

I have always been a great admirer of Athabasca University, a Canadian leader in distance education based in Alberta. For ten years I was a board member of the university's governing council, and for six years the chair of the MBA program in the Centre for Innovative Management. I learned a great deal. Some Athabasca University students are Native young people living throughout Canada, some in isolated areas where distance education is a necessity. When I attend the graduation ceremonies, and listen to the students' testimonials, I am always moved by the enormous struggles many of them have had to overcome to earn their degrees. Some have large families, some have disabilities, yet they persevere. On June 8, 2006, I was very proud to be the first recipient of the Order of Athabasca, an award which recognizes exemplary service to the university. Yet I am prouder of those determined students who have reached their goals and realized their dreams.

NorQuest College is another post-secondary institution in Edmonton that has helped countless Native students pursue their education as adults. In 2005 NorQuest named the Belcourt auditorium after me, an honour I appreciate because I admire the college's innovative approach and its achievements. The college makes an extraordinary effort to provide a welcoming environment for Native people, including an Aboriginal Ceremonial Room. These endeavours will not be forgotten.

For the past four years I have served as one of the RCMP Commanding Officer's Aboriginal Advisors for K Division in Alberta. Our task is to act as a liaison between the RCMP and aboriginal communities. This has been another learning experience for me, because I had not previously realized the challenges that all communities face through illegal drugs, alcohol abuse, and violence.

I have a great deal of respect for the RCMP so I have appreciated this opportunity for direct involvement. I have recently been invited to become a member of the Edmonton Police Foundation to support the city police in creating a safer community.

As a businessman, I have a natural interest in encouraging Métis young people to go into business. When I was on the board of Apeetogosan, we did a lot of marketing in this area. Ron Stevens, our CEO, did a super job. His background was in banking which was really helpful. We set up an arm of Apeetogosan called Pinnacle which helped clients prepare a business plan and a loan application. When the loan was approved, Apeetogosan would provide the clients with accounting services.

Community work is important to me. I have done a lot of fundraising for the arts and service clubs such as the Lions, Rotary, Canadian Club, and the Shriners. They make a great contribution to our society, and need volunteers.

I HAVE A few goals on my list, too, although I am an older man now.

First, I want to work hard to convince the Alberta government, the Canadian government, private industry, and hundreds of individuals to match the funds in the Belcourt Brosseau Métis Awards so that many thousands of young Métis students across western Canada can reach the educational goals they set for themselves.

Second, I want to see all Native people—the Métis and the First Nations—work together to achieve justice in this country. Sometimes I think that the reason Canative Housing thrived was that Georges, Orval, and I stuck

Returning to Lac Ste. Anne, I can touch the past.

together, no matter how many arrows came at us, and that is why we succeeded. Each one of us had different views, but we stuck together. That is the secret. Governments like to divide Native people, and they have done that so successfully: throwing a carrot here, and another carrot there, a little piece of meat on the bone here, and another piece there. They do this to keep people happy for a while—or to keep them fighting with one another.

The day the Native people get together—the First Nations and the Métis—and stand together, do you realize what would happen? We would stand up for what is fair, and governments would have to listen and act accordingly.

When I was a child, they labelled us "half-breeds." What a terrible stigma to place on a child! I felt so dirty. I didn't know what the words meant. *Indian. Dirty half-breed.* I remember those words. Later, I felt as if I had been caught between two worlds. As I matured, I started to understand that being Métis gave me a double advantage. I have learned from both the Aboriginal and European cultures, and I have used what I have learned to my advantage.

I look back on all of this, and I am proud of who I am. I am proud of the Métis people, and I want them to be proud of themselves. Failure is not in my vocabulary. It shouldn't be in anyone's vocabulary. We will succeed if we work together.

Finally, I want to live long enough to see people take care of this beautiful country we have inherited from our ancestors. We cannot keep depleting the earth. This is where we need to go back to the traditions of the Native people of early Alberta. They regarded all life as sacred. If they took something from the earth, they replaced it. They saw interconnections among all the forms of life.

We have lost that ability. Our ancestors knew that if you interfere with the natural cycle of life, something goes wrong. Today, we see many imbalances caused by human interference, often motivated by greed, but more often by ignorance. Today in Alberta, few people are in touch with nature. Walk in the country, lean with your back against a tree, and breathe in the energy from that tree. You will be surprised at how invigorated you will feel. You will have no need for artificial drugs or alcohol. Alone in nature, away from the constant noise of society, with its ringing cellphones and blaring music, a person can be healed.

The Native people knew that once, but many have lost that knowledge. I rediscovered it as I walked through the woods at Lac Ste. Anne, searching for something I had never lost. Go for your own walk in the woods, and find your own trail to your past, and to your future. You are rich. Everything you need, you already have.

Belcourt Family Stories

EARLY LIFE IN LAC STE. ANNE IN THE 1870S
by Victoria Belcourt Callihoo

Victoria Belcourt was born in 1861, a granddaughter of Joseph Belcourt, the voyageur who founded our family with his Métis wife, Catherine L'Hirondelle. Victoria was the daughter of Alexis Belcourt and Nancy Rowand, and through her mother, she was the granddaughter of Archange Nipissing and Antoine Rowand, and a great-granddaughter of Louise Umfreville and John Rowand, the chief factor for the Hudson's Bay Company at Fort Edmonton.

In 1878, when she was seventeen, Victoria married Louis Jerome Callihoo of Lac Ste. Anne, and the couple raised thirteen children. In 1948, she gave a series of oral history interviews about early life in the community, which were published in the Alberta Historical Review in 1953 and 1956. They are reprinted here with permission. Victoria Belcourt Callihoo died in 1966.

OUR HOUSES WERE made of hewn spruce logs, mostly. We had only two windows in them, no upper floors, no glass, but a rawhide skin of a calf, deer, or moose calf was used. Only the hair would be taken off. It was put on the window while wet, and nailed on with wooden pegs on slats around the window. When dry, it would be taut and might be used as a drum. It was not transparent, but gave light. Though not as good as glass, it had one advantage. No peeping Tom was going to peep through your window. Therefore, window blinds were unnecessary.

We had saws about eight feet long—they looked like ice saws—with handles at each end. A platform was built about ten feet above the ground. A log would be hoisted up and a man on top would pull the saw up, the one below would pull the saw down, sawing the log on the downward stroke. Lots of floors were made of hewn logs placed tightly together. Even doors were made of hewn logs. All the tools were supplied by the H.B. Co. (Hudson's Bay Company) store. Rafters were made of poles about three feet apart. Most of the roofs were one-quarter pitch. Then the builder would go into the forest to get bark from the spruce trees, the bark being taken off the tree during sapping time. The length of the bark would be six feet or so, and the width varied according to the size of the tree. This bark, after it was taken off the tree, would be set flat on rails above the ground to dry. I may say now that the very best of timber was within a mile from the settlements, for there were no loose fires in those days to destroy and mar nature's picture. When the bark was dry in the fall, it was then laid on the rafters, lapping on top like shingles. The bark

Brooms made by Victoria Belcourt Callihoo, on display in
the Lac Ste. Anne Historical Society Pioneer Museum.
PHOTO APPEARS COURTESY OF THE MUSÉE HERITAGE ST. ALBERT

was then pinned down with long poles crosswise from
the roof. Holes were bored in the pole and pins made of
wood were driven tight, thus making a leak-proof roof.
The outer bark was laid outside. The inside roof was
therefore smooth and glossy.

As there were no stoves, open fireplaces were built in
either corner from the door. We called these mud stoves.
They were made of poles, mud and hay mixed, and more
mud and water, making a smooth finish. White clay was
then mixed in water and rubbed all over with a cloth.
When dry, this was white. Usually, two iron bars were
hung about four feet from the floor. These bars were
used to hang kettles on. We got these bars from the H.B.
store and also from old discarded guns. About a foot
away from the mud stove, the floor was plastered down
solid, and precaution taken so sparks would not ignite
and burn the house. The open chimney was built about

two feet above the roof, so the sparks would not drop on the roof. On a windy night, sparks could be seen coming out thick, but the chimney being high, they would drop to the ground harmlessly. The house was then chinked, plastered with clay, white-mud washed, a cellar door was made in the floor, and the house was ready to move into.

But before the house had been occupied two days, the owner had to invite the neighbours to a big dance. We danced reels, jigs, and other old-time dances. We had not tables; because we didn't have them, we didn't miss them; no chairs or benches. We ate on the floor. A canvas was spread with a white cloth on top; then the set was ready for the meal. We had a three-corner cupboard in a corner for our dishes. A cloth was hung over, for the lumber was scarce and hard to make. We got strap-hinges and latches from the Posts. Others had wooden latches and wooden hinges. A hole was bored in a slab or board and another slab, with a tongue in the end, would serve as a hinge. They were very squeaky. Our pots and dishes were from the H.B. Co. The pots were made of copper and they were seamless. We had eight gallons to two-pint pots. They were very useful and stood rough usage. When a pot was bumped, it was easy to hammer back to its proper shape.

There were no beds; everyone slept on the floor. All bedding was gathered, folded, and placed in one corner of the house in the daytime. Big pieces of slab wood would be placed, standing up (perpendicular), on the mud stove. Usually, coals of fire would still be burn-ing until morning. The fire from the mud stove would give a glow, providing both heat and light. We had not lamps, nor candles, so after a few years we made our own candles. Our bedding consisted of duck and goose feather for mattresses and pillows, and buffalo robes and H.B. Co. four-point blankets.

We had no flour. We grew a little barley. We cut a block of black poplar, about thirty inches high and sixteen inches in diameter. We bored a hole about six to eight inches deep and seven across. We would soak the barley in lukewarm water for a while, drain off the water, and pour the barley into this block. We had a hammer-like apparatus that just fitted this, with which we pounded the barley in the hole for about twenty minutes. In that time, the hulls would be all off the grain. We separated the hulls from the grain and used the grain for soup, which was wholesome and delicious. When the grain was very dry, we put it in a frying pan, adding a little grease, and when cooked brown, it was a good substitute for bread. We had no coffee, but again barley came to the rescue. We put the barley in the frying-pan, without hulling it, and when it was fired really black, we used that for coffee. We had tea and block sugar, like we had during the war in the cafés.

Though the buffalo had now gone, we raised cattle, hogs, and chickens. Food was still plentiful as moose, deer, and bear were plentiful. We then turned to these animals for food and clothing. Moose hide, when tanned, made nice moccasins and coats, pants, mitts, gloves, and other articles, but it never made a robe—the hair came off too easily, and the same with the deer. We began raising cattle, and in the fall, we butchered one, or sometimes two, to carry us through the winter. Some of the Métis didn't care for beef at first, but they soon got over that.

A beaded vest made by Victoria Belcourt Callihoo,
on display at the Musée Heritage in St. Albert.
PHOTO APPEARS COURTESY OF THE MUSÉE HERITAGE ST. ALBERT

We got thread from the H.B. Co. store and we learned
to make our own nets. We had lots of fish—we were never
short of food.

We milked cows. We made our own milk pans out of
birch bark. We used tiny long roots, which we got in the
muskegs, to sew the pans and berry pots with. We used
spruce gum heated to close the seams and leaks of the
birch pans. Birch canoes were made the same way. They
were very light.

We barbequed fish, fowl, and large pieces of meat
over the open fire, or covered the bird, feathers and
all, under hot coals of wood, and this cooked wonder-
fully, and you ate something that was never touched by
anyone. Potatoes were cooked the same way and had
good flavour.

Métis from Lac Ste. Anne and St. Albert often visited each other, that is, once or twice a year. Their two settlements were of the same people, and they were related mostly. There would be a man or a family from Lac La Biche or Slave Lake who would come and live in the settlement. The two settlements were all Catholics, L'Hirondelle, Belcourt, Gladus, Plante, Laderoute, and Gauthier, and were of French descent. Letendres' ancestors came from the Beaver Indians in the Peace River country; around forty years ago, a lot of these people went up to Grande Prairie, where trapping and hunting was good.

Our clothing was from cloth brought in by the H.B. Co. Our men never had underwear, nor socks—there weren't any—but we had large overcoats from Buffalo skins, and outer leggings were worn, made from H.B. Co. blankets. These leggings reached up to the waist. A buckskin string was tied to the legging and that tied to one's belt. Women also had no stockings. Like the men, they wrapped their feet with an oblong piece of flannel. Women wore leggings. They were worn below the knee. They were made of black velvet and were beaded on one side, the outside of the leg. When we women did outside work, or made trips in winter, we wrapped our knees with flannelette. Women had no coats, but wore shawls.

Our livestock consisted of horses, cattle, pigs, and chickens, all scrubs.

During the buffalo hunts, some settler would go on through to Red River for supplies that weren't available here. They would bring back ploughs, garden tools, and tubs. They would return in the fall, and usually two families or more would come back with them to settle out here. These families came in wagons. (Firewater) whiskey would be brought in from Winnipeg, and rum and brandy were sold or bartered by the H.B. Co.

We had no soap, but we made *la potash* from fats or grease with ashes and lye. We used it for our toilet and washing soap. Perhaps it was rather hard for the delicate skin, but it was as good as any soap I have used. Some of us still use *la potash* to this day.

No brooms were to be had at the store. We made them out of a certain kind of willow. We chose the long taper kind. These sticks were taken from the tops, about two feet long. About one hundred of these would be tied together around a four-foot smooth stick—this was the broom handle. The stick was driven into the centre of the tied willows, and our broom was ready for use.

Moss was pulled up in the fall, after haying. Little spruce trees were cut halfway, about two feet from the ground, and the upper part pushed down, and we put our moss on top of this sort of rack, where it would dry before winter set in. It was hauled in as needed. Moss was a household necessity. We raised our babies with it. We stuffed it in moss bags in which our babies were laced up. We did not use any diapers. We used moss to wipe floors after scrubbing them.

We cultivated our land—an acre or two—with a ten-inch plough. An ox would be trained to pull it. The ox was used in around the place and for hauling hay, but the ponies were used for fast travelling, as going to weddings and dances, and in case of sickness, to get the priest. When ploughing was done, a wooden harrow was then dragged on the ploughed land, usually a boy leading the horses. The seeds were sown broadcast. Fences were made of rails laid on blocks. The oxen and horses were driven singly. We had no double harness.

Our hogs were spotted, black and white. They were brought by boat up river by the H.B. Co. Our haying equivalent was an Armstrong mower (scythe), wooden fork with wooden prongs, which were rather cumbersome. When the hay was dry, it was gathered with forks and cocked. We had no hay-rakes. When all the hay was cocked, it was left to settle for a few days, and it was brought in by men with two poles. These poles were shoved under the cock, about two feet apart, then the whole cock would be lifted clean and brought to the stack. Round hay stacks were put up. We had no hay racks. Small racks were built on long-runner sleighs, a sort of stone box. Oxen hauled the hay home in winter.

Of course, we had dog trains too, for faster trips. One didn't care when one left for a trip with a dog team, morning, noon, or evening. My husband left Lac Ste. Anne in the evening and arrived at the "House," Edmonton, before sunrise the following morning.

After the hunts were over, some people went down to Morley or *man-a-chap-pan-nihh* (meaning "where the bows were taken"). This is how Bow River got its name, which is wrong. Bow River in Indian is "*ask-ka-we-see pee*," which means "Don't-freeze-over-river;" this river was never known to be frozen over all winter for ponies crossing it.

Better and cheaper horses were later brought up from the Blackfeet of the Old Man's River.

We bartered our furs at the H.B. Co. Usually the Company advanced a settler with credit after haying, and on through the year until the trapper brought in his catch. Often, the fur would pay more than the debt the settler owed, and the Store would pay him. He would draw this, off and on. As there was no money, this transaction was called "Fur." So much fur for this, so much fur for the other article. Later on, when the Indian Commissioners came to pay treaty money (late 1870s and 1880s), money began to circulate. It seemed more confusing to deal in money when one was accustomed to barter. I have heard of some Indians trading a used five-dollar bill for a brand new dollar bill.

We used to see Battle River people, off and on. Since they were Métis of French extraction like us, good fellowship prevailed, and some marriages took place. We did not come in contact with the Métis at Victoriam their being of Anglo-Saxon descent and of a different denomination, no visits, to my knowledge, were ever made to them.

OUR BUFFALO HUNTS
by Victoria Belcourt Callihoo

I was thirteen years old when I first joined in a buffalo hunt. We left Lac Ste. Anne after the leaves were out on the poplar trees and our small fields and gardens were seeded or planted. Before making the journey, there would be a meeting among the leading men as to the exact day of leaving. After this was decided on, all the families who wanted to join the hunt would prepare for the trip. Our main transportation, the Red River cart, would be overhauled. These vehicles at the time did not have any metal in their construction. Large wooden pegs were used where bolts would be used now, while small pegs answered for screws or nails. Cart harness was made of hides from the buffalo.

I always used to accompany my mother on these trips. She was a medicine woman who set broken bones and knew how to use medicinal herbs. The riders who chased the buffalo were often thrown, sometimes by the bulls charging the riders' horses or by the horses getting their feet in badger holes.

We usually took three carts along. We had no axle grease, and tallow was used instead to lubricate the wooden axles. The carts were very squeaky and they could be heard from a long way off.

We, from Lac Ste. Anne, would be the first to start as we were the furthest north. The Métis of St. Albert settlement would join us on the way. Usually, there would be about one hundred families going on the hunt. All the streams were forded, as there were no bridges. The Saskatchewan River was the largest and most dangerous, and it was a relief after it was crossed. We used to cross at a good ford about where the High Level Bridge is now. About a day's travel south from Saskatchewan River, we usually found the herd. Riders, young men they were, would scout on ahead to see we did not run into any enemies. There were no police—no law. We always had a leader in our caravan, and his orders were respected. He always had a flag flying on top of his cart. He led his people ahead and we followed him.

When the herd was startled, it was just a dark solid moving mass. We, of those days, never could believe the buffalo would ever be killed off, for there were thousands and thousands. We took firewood and poles for tipis and for tripods, on which we hung our thin sliced slab meat to dry in the sun. We had no matches, but got fire from flint and birch punk. It seems no one was anxious to start their morning fire, as we would wait and see if any smoke would come out of the tipis, and when smoke was seen, then there was a rush to get a flame or coal to start one's own fire.

The riders of the chase all had guns, single barrel flint locks—some muzzle-loaders with caps. Bows and arrows were used before my time, but the Crees and Blackfeet still used them then. Powder horns and ball rags were slung on each shoulder. At close range, the guns would kill the animal. Some riders rode bareback, while others had homemade saddles. They were almost flat and were stuffed with the hair of the buffalo. They were beaded on the corners, and stirrups were of dry rawhide. When the kill was over, the women would go out to help bring the meat in, and then the slicing of the meat began. We girls would then keep a little smoke going all day to keep the flies away from the meat. The meat would be hung on rails that rested on two tripods at each end.

Often we would run short of wood. Then a pony would be hitched to a cart and we would go out on the plain and pick chips (buffalo dung). On a warm day, this was very dry and burned readily. Only the old ones were used for fuel. The buffalo was a very useful animal, for we ate the meat, we used its hide for robes, shelter for our lodges, footwear, clothes, and bags. The meat was cooked and sun-dried and also made into pemmican. We always camped close to water. We set our tipis in a large circle outside the cart circle. A few of the fastest horses were kept in this enclosure, and the others were herded all night by a night herder, for horse thieving was a very common occurrence. A fast horse was the best possession. A hunter on a fast horse would kill more buffalo than others with less speedy ponies. There was no money; no one knew what it was.

We made pemmican out on the plains, as the dried meat was too bulky to take home. A large green hide would be hung on six posts, three on each side, so the hide would form a U-shape. When it was dry, the slabs of meat would be dumped in the U-shaped hide and two men on each end would then pound the dry meat into a pulp. Then sun-dried saskatoons would be mixed and grease would be poured on and stirred to make an even mixture. When this was done, it would be packed in robes, sewn with sinew all around, the hair part outside to keep the pemmican in good condition regardless of the weather. These bags were heavy, and it usually took two men to load one on a cart. Hides would be put on top of the loads. Nothing would be wasted from the buffalo but the bones, hoofs, and horns. The fall hunt, the last before winter, which would start after haying, was the most important one, for we had to get enough dried meat and pemmican to last all winter. At this time, the buffalo would be fat and calves grown up. Calves were not killed, as no one cared for veal anyway.

The homeward journey was slow, but who cared? The nice sunny days in the fall, Indian summer, made travelling rather fascinating. Occasionally we would run into bad weather, but we were accustomed to it and did not mind, as long as we had plenty of the best and most nourishing food I ever ate. In all, I made four trips to the plains hunting the buffalo. Each was further away toward south.

VOICE OVER WATER

Lesley Tarrant Belcourt captures the flavour of life at Lac Ste. Anne in the late 1930s and early 1940s in this original story about her husband's family.

"Game wardens are coming!" they shout in Cree across the lake, and my dad knows that Mr. Forsland from the Alberta Game Branch has phoned the store at Lac St. Anne. And I know that all he has said is, "Say Mr. Forsland called," for the cry to go out along the banks of Alberta Beach. Then out-of-season, bootlegged muskrats are stuffed into the false bottom of our kitchen table. All the younger kids are lying scared in bed, except me, when they finally burst in around midnight, trying to catch Dad red-handed. They can't find anything, though. Just water boiling on the wood stove for tea and Mom sewing us kids new shirts from sugar sacks, while Dad and old Father Calvez smoke and play rummy. Dad pretends to look surprised when they walk in, as if Rex hasn't already barked before they reach the porch.

"Working late tonight," Dad says, calm-like, looking up from his cards. "Sure wouldn't want you guys' jobs."

"Tea?" Mom already has two filled mugs on the table. But they wander around first, prodding here and there, lifting lids, opening doors—the usual search before tea and cards.

"Don't know how you do it, Wilfred," says the tall one. "You're a cunning bastard." And Dad shuffles the cards and the four of them play rummy at that same table, their smoke-hidden heads inches above the muskrats, until the teapot is empty. They finally leave when Father Calvez stretches and mentions Mass in the morning. Chairs scrape. And the table is empty, except for scattered cards, twisted butts, mug rings, and those invisible muskrats.

"That's right," says Dad. "You get those sinners to go to church and give you their money, Father, so I can win it all back." And he laughs. The wardens laugh, too, because they don't know that it's really Dad's I-got-one-over-on-you-guys laugh. The sound of their heavy shoes disappears underneath Rex's bark, as they march down the porch steps into the long grass, slamming truck doors, beaming lights across our windows. Then they are gone, until next time.

When the fur-buyer Albert Cadre passes through Lac St. Anne, he always stops to see Dad. He's kind of sweet on Dad's sister, Auntie Christina, too. Albert isn't a regular half-breed like the rest of us. Dad tells us he's Syrian. But he says it in a way that makes us think he must be special.

"That guy, he's got lots of money," Dad says, "because he only pays me five cents a skin." And I know Dad admires him for that—for having money, not for paying him so little.

When I take Dad's lunch pail out to where he's grubbing stumps for Old Man Petersen, he's already sitting, and looking across the brown stubble field. He pats my head in that absent way he does when he's thinking.

"You know, son," he says, still looking at the wide sky ahead, "I think I'll sell to the city. Cut out the middleman. That'll give Cadre something to think about." And he opens his pail and eats lunch.

That night, Dad plays rummy with Father Calvez again on top of the rats. I'm in bed with the other kids, even though it's Saturday, but I hear them through the wall, Father's wheezy laugh and Dad's cry, "More tea, Florence," and truck doors slamming in the distance. I must have fallen asleep, because I remember only Father's voice, as he steps onto the porch; "I'd better see you at Mass for this, Wilfred."

The next morning is Sunday, and we usually go with Gran to Mass. Sometimes I'm an altar boy. Gran sees to that. We take the horses and buggy instead of walking three miles, like for school, and I listen to the bells jingling on the harness and watch the brushed manes flying behind the proud heads. But today Dad comes, too. He's wearing a clean shirt and his hair is smoothed with Brylcreem and his glasses shine.

Father Calvez is greeting everyone at the front door of the white wooden building with its stained-glass window and the wooden cross on the roof. We walk up the front steps.

"Well, Wilfred," says Father Calvez in a voice loud enough for an Easter pageant. "This is a pleasant surprise." And Old Lady Letendre in front turns and gives a smirk. "And to what do we owe the pleasure?" Dad looks out of place without a smoke.

"Well, Father, I heard your sermons were so good, I couldn't stay away," says Dad.

They shake hands and continue to smile—Dad through the whole service, it seems. Even when the collection plate is passed around, he smiles, opening his tightly clenched fist over the brass platter and jingling us into surprise. He doesn't close his eyes, but stares at the altar, until Father Calvez finally wafts incense over us at the Blessing and allows us to go home. That evening, Father Calvez is back, playing rummy in the kitchen.

"I should charge you, you know, Wilfred."

"For what?"

"For all the extra incense required to cover the smell of those muskrats!"

And they both laugh I-got-one-over-on-everybody laughs. And Dad knocks on the table. It makes an empty, hollow echo.

"I always knew that altar of yours could be put to good use," says Dad.

"Now, now Wilfred." Father Calvez becomes more serious. "It's only help for a good friend. If I can't hide a few gunny sacks of muskrats from the thieving government, what am I good for?"

But Dad's new hiding place is short-lived. One of the Brothers brings Father Calvez the news that someone has discovered the muskrats at the back of the altar. Shortly after, a voice carries over the water in Cree, "Game wardens are coming." Dad has no ideas left. He smokes a lot and waits until long past midnight, but nobody arrives.

"It's alright, Wilfred," says Father Calvez the next morning. "One of the Brothers moved the sacks through the back of the church into the barn-loft before they started searching. But we can't keep them there indefinitely. I think you'll have to get them to the city soon."

Dad is getting worried, though.

"You know, Florence," he says to Mom, "I don't think we should hide them here anymore. We'll have to think of somewhere else." And I know from his voice that he's already thought of somewhere, but he's not going to tell yet. The problem, he says, is getting the rats to the city. There's not just the problem of smuggling them from the kitchen table into the Ford. What if the wardens stop him on the road?

"Cream cans," he says slowly. "That's it. Cream cans."

We load the cream cans onto the Ford that afternoon, just before Albert Cadre arrives.

"You want to sell rats?" asks Albert.

"Got a better buyer," lies Dad. "Giving me ten cents. You sell them for more."

"No way."

"Damn liar. How can you buy mine for five cents and still make a living?" And Dad and I, we both get in the truck and head into the city with the cream-cans, leaving Cadre shaking his head.

On the way, we see two reserve Indians thumbing. There's not enough room in a 1938 Ford for all of us in the cab, so one gets in the back and sits with the cream cans. It's when we get to about 109th Street and Jasper Avenue that Dad makes a sudden stop. One of the cream cans topples over, and the lid falls off. The Indian tries to catch the falling can, thinking it's full of cream, but to his surprise, out spill Dad's muskrats. We scoop them up as fast as we can and put the lid back on. The Indian says nothing, but after he gets out, Dad says he knows he was sure thinking. And I know Dad's thinking, too, about how he'll probably have to find another way to get the rats to the city next time.

That night when we're back home, Dad can't stop talking about it to Mom. Not only about the muskrats spilling out.

"You could've knocked me over, Florence," he says, lighting up a smoke. "I said ten cents and they said okay, just like that. Ten cents. We've doubled our money,

Florence. Ten cents a rat." It doesn't take Dad long to work out something else.

"Now what the hell is that bastard Cadre getting? Must be more than ten."

Albert is back the next day.

"I've been thinking," he says. "I think I can find ten cents for your rats. It'll break me, of course. But what are friends for?"

"No," says Dad. "Seems I can get twenty cents in the city."

"Twenty!"

"Sure thing." Dad jingles some coins in his pocket, like it's proof.

Albert pauses. "Fifteen. I'll give you fifteen."

"Fifteen?"

"Yeah, fifteen."

Dad puffs his smoke a few times and looks into the distance, like he's thinking hard. "Boy, Cadre, you sure strike a hard bargain. I'm gonna lose, but what the hell, you're almost a brother. Fifteen it is." And they shake hands.

For the next few months, Dad smuggles muskrats into the city in the cream cans. It seems as if the Indian hasn't reported him after all. Each time, Dad gets a higher price for the rats.

"Only fifteen?" he asks the city buyer. "I can get twenty at Alberta Beach."

On the way home from his last visit, he has his foot pressed hard on the gas all the way. "Wait till I see Cadre!" he says with excitement. "Just wait."

Albert comes two weeks later.

"Here," he says to Dad. "Fifteen cents a rat."

Dad knows Albert can't afford to buy his muskrats anymore.

"Sorry," says Dad. "I'm getting twenty now."

"Twenty!"

"Twenty. A couple weeks ago, they gave me twenty."

"That's what I'm getting for them!" And Cadre pulls all his money out of his pockets, throws it on the ground, and jumps up and down on it.

"Money is your God," he yells. "Money is your God!"

From then on, Albert sells his furs to my dad. And my dad becomes the fur buyer. And shortly after that, Albert marries Auntie Christina.

But then a voice carries over the water again.

"Seems like that Indian reported me after all," says Dad to Father Calvez when they next meet in the kitchen for cards and tea.

"Maybe," says Father, looking at his hand, "you need to go into another business."

"Another business?" And I can tell Dad is pleased to hear his dealing called business.

"Yes, Wilfred. Diversify."

"Like what?"

"John Letendre brews moonshine, you know."

"Moonshine?"

"Just something else to fall back on," says Father Calvez.

And Dad nods slowly and puffs on his smoke.

But how my dad beat John Letendre at making moonshine is another story that will have to wait till next time, because right now a voice carries over the water. "Game wardens are coming."

Suggestions for Further Reading

Healing Waters: The pilgrimage to Lac Ste. Anne, by Steve Simon [Edmonton: University of Alberta Press, 1995].

Lac Ste-Anne Sakahigan, by E.M. Drouin [Edmonton: Editions de l'Ermitage, 1973].

The First Metis, A New Nation, by Anne Anderson [Edmonton, Uvisco Press, 1985].

The Sun Traveller: The Story of the Callihoos in Alberta, by Elizabeth MacPherson [St. Albert: Musée Heritage, 2003].

Métis Legacy: a Métis historiography and annotated bibliography, edited by Lawrence Barkwell, Leah Dorion and Darren Prefontaine [Winnipeg: Pemmican Publications, 2001].

Aboriginal Cultures in Alberta: Five Hundred Generations, by Susan Berry and Jack Brink, [Edmonton: Provincial Museum of Alberta, 2004].

Acknowledgements

I AM DEEPLY GRATEFUL TO MY wife, Lesley, not only for her unqualified, dedicated support as I wrote this book, and for the many late nights she spent transcribing my taped words, but for understanding my need to pursue my dreams, for giving me confidence in myself, and for being there when I needed her.

Special thanks to my brother Gordon, who shared with me his enormous collection of research documents and photographs, and helped me get to know him better.

My thanks to the many people who provided me with invaluable material, including my nine siblings—Ken, Gilbert, Georgina, Gordon, Virginia, Marie, Josephine, Viola, and Patsy—who shared not only their photographs but also their memories, and helped jog mine; and to my cousin Bob Belcourt and childhood friend Harvey (Chapps) Letendre for lending me photos.

I am honoured that Audrey Poitras, President of the Métis Nation of Alberta, has written the foreword to this book. Her foresight and vision for the cultural education of Métis people has been an inspiration.

I am grateful to Orval Belcourt and Georges Brosseau, who have been my partners in an inspirational, unique, and successful endeavour, Canative Housing Corporation, and subsequently the Belcourt Brosseau Métis Awards. Thank you to Orval for guidance on social services matters, to Georges for answering my questions regarding the legal system, and to both gentlemen for putting up with me.

My thanks to David Holehouse for his vast research and early writing of a book originally intended to be about Canative Housing Corporation. I remain hopeful that we can resurrect this project sometime in the near future. Sincere thanks to Brian Tod for thirty-five years of friendship and legal advice, from the incorporation of Belcourt Construction to the formation of the Belcourt Brosseau Métis Awards.

I am indebted to all those other dear friends who listened patiently to my stories over coffee and who constantly encouraged me to write them down. Danny Bonko encouraged me to put words down on paper. Louise Hayes offered constant support and suggested I write my story, not just the Canative Housing story. Chuck Neher gave his continuing friendship, encouragement, and brainstorming sessions. Al Benson filled my memory lapses with information. Don Enyedy, Ihor Bayduza, and Ray Masuda urged me to share my stories with others, and not just with them. I am also grateful to my companions at Tim Horton's on Baseline Road in Sherwood Park, and to the Ardrossan Seniors, for laughing with me as I told them some of my stories.

Special thanks to my cousin Tony Belcourt for being a true pioneer and scout, leading me to this less-travelled path; to Gene Rheaume, Walter Rudnicki, Louise Hayes, and the late Gordon Hornby for inspiring me to take this walk through the woods; and to my good friend Senator Orville Phillips, who offered me a challenge I could not refuse.

Thanks to my dear grandchildren, Amethyst and Azlan, for helping me choose the right title for this book, and for accompanying me on my journey through the woods for the rest of my life.

I would like to thank Ruth Linka of Brindle & Glass for believing in this book, even before it was finished, and for accepting it for publication.

This book has benefited enormously from the clear, precise editing of Linda Goyette. My special thanks to Linda for her generous assistance, thoughtful advice, and enthusiastic encouragement that this was a project worth doing.